SECRETS OF THE PATAGONIAN BARBECUE

ROBERTO MARÍN

ORIGO

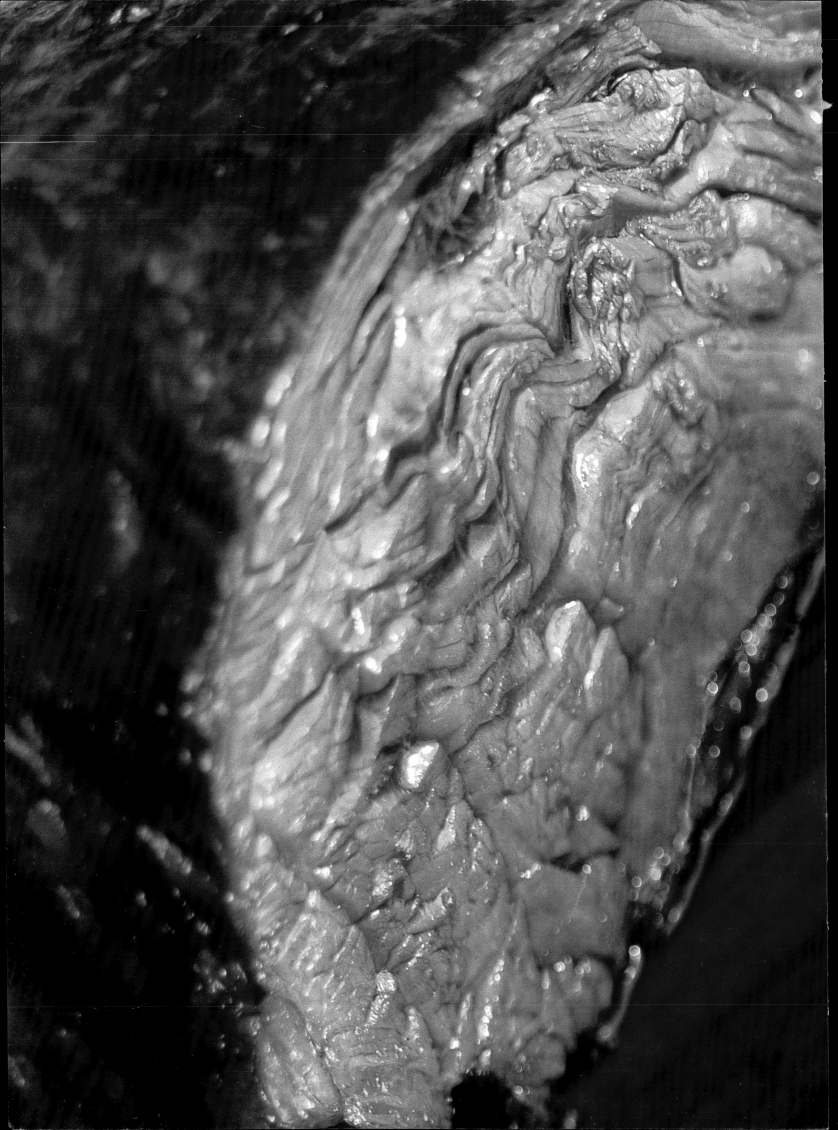

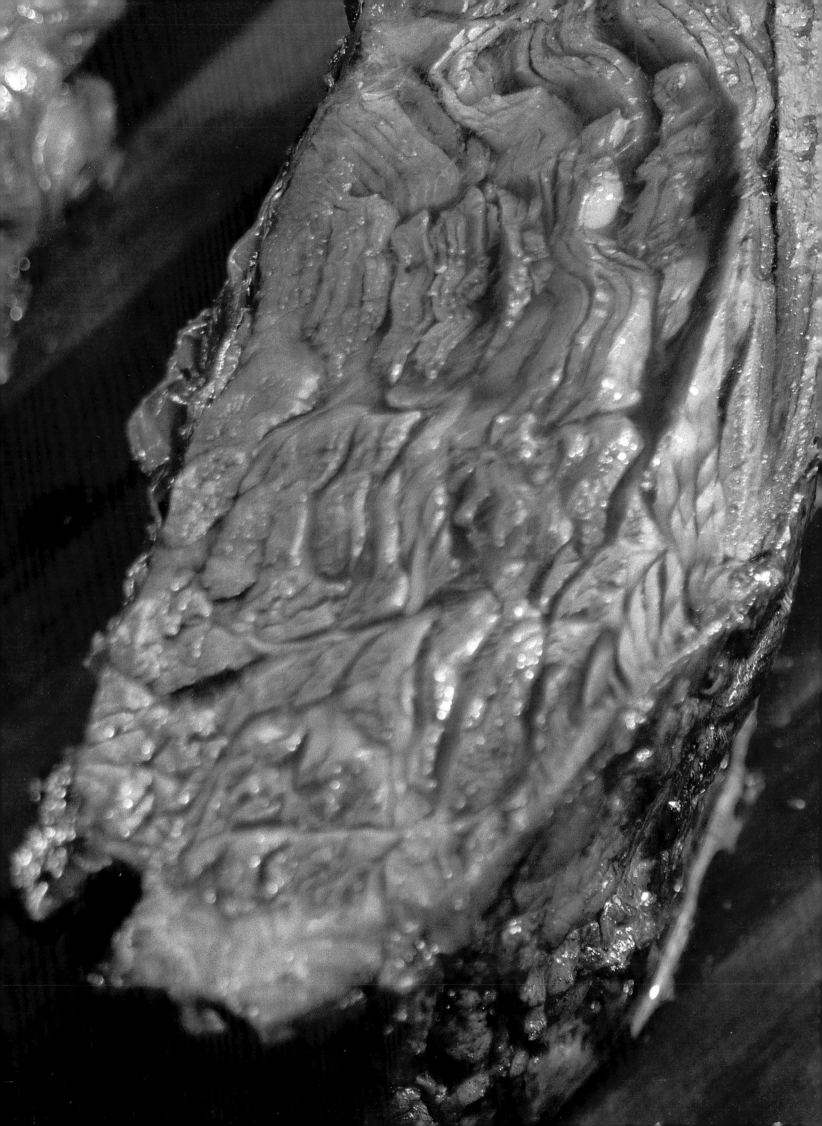

CONTENTS

Secrets of the Patagonian Barbecue is the result of a lifetime of experience and gastronomical culture of three great masters of the ancient art of the grill. Read, learn, and enjoy. Take your moments of relaxation seriously, and remember the words of the ancient Romans so many centuries ago: Leisure with dignity!

INTRODUCTION

GRILLING: A MAN'S WORLD

Americans love grilling. All Americans, from Canada to Patagonia, consider the art of the barbecue a firmly-established and dearly-loved tradition. And let's face it, whenever a grill is fired up in Latin America, a group of men is sure to gather around it. Throughout history its inhabitants, whether indigenous, colonists, immigrants, or native sons, have met regularly at the grill. These gastronomical gatherings have been the ideal pretext for initiating and strengthening close friendships, just as our distant ancestors did thousands of years ago during their extended hunting trips. But humans have not always been enthusiastic carnivores; that characteristic was developed over time and only after very long periods of abstinence. This is the story of how men became carnivores, hunters, and finally, grillers.

Our most distant ancestors were happy enough just to survive, and they ate whatever was available: fruits, seeds, leaves, shoots, and herbs, etc. Proteins were provided by eggs and small, easily-caught animals. When this wasn't enough – and it often wasn't – they were quite willing to complement their diet with any bug that happened by.

Safely observing from a prudent distance, our primitive man envied the large, fierce, hunting animals that easily brought down their prey and earned their right to leisurely gnaw on the fresh, juicy flesh of their prize until they had had their fill. As the contented beasts sauntered away, our man continued to watch, this time with contempt, as the site filled with packs of hyenas, jackals, or other wild dogs who greedily squabbled over the remaining scraps. Once the carrion-eating dogs scattered, our man finally had his turn to approach the ravaged remains. Only then could he attack the skeleton with his stone mallet to get at the marrow and brains.

And so man became a devoted carnivore, a dedicated fanatic of meat, although his access to it was limited and always dependent upon the good fortune of stumbling onto some beast devouring its prey. He found ways to turn his primitive wood, stone, and bone tools into implements for hunting small animals and finally gained access to fresh meat. And so began the first division of labor; men became hunters and left the women of the tribe to the business of gathering food, which ensured survival during times when game was scarce.

Our hunter advanced in his weapons-making ability over time and he moved on to crafting arrowheads and spears. Soon the men of the tribe organized hunting parties in order to bring down large herbivores such as buffalos, mastodons, and mammoths. The adventure of hunting and the well-earned rewards bestowed upon them by the women upon their return to the tribe with one of their trophies added to the desire for meat and led them to develop the first trade: hunting.

GOOD TIMES AND A RELAXED ATMOSPHERE GENERATE LIVELY CONVERSATION AND PLENTY OF OPINIONS. THOSE GATHERED AROUND THE GRILL HAPPILY MAKE COMMENTS AND OFFER ADVICE, REGARDLESS OF THEIR DEGREE OF KNOWLEDGE OF THIS CULINARY ART, CONFIRMING THE THEORY THAT YOU CAN MAKE A CHEF, BUT A GRILLER IS BORN TO HIS CRAFT.

Some 600,000 years ago early man experienced a major cultural turning point: he learned to keep and manage the fire that was generated by lightening. This allowed him to develop elementary culinary techniques to cook food over flames and coals, under hot ashes, and on top of hot rocks. The great joy that spread around the campfire as they roasted a deer or a piece of mammoth meat and the well-earned recognition received by the new hunter-griller began to shape this new trade into a decidedly male pursuit. This simple way of cooking so satisfied the culinary demands of the times that 590,000 years went by without any significant changes in cooking methods. That only occurred 10,000 years ago, with the advent of pottery.

Customs have a way of changing and adapting to their times, but some things continue to stand firm. While "machismo" may no longer be the fully-tolerated tradition it once was when groups gathered around the barbecue grill, the term Grill "Master" continues to be a masculine title for what remains a predominately male activity.

THE PATAGONIAN METHOD

Open-air grills generate excitement and high spirits among friends and families all around the world, but it goes beyond that in Patagonia, where grilling ranks among the pillars of cultural idolatry, right next to soccer. But this reverence for the grill hardly makes every enthusiast adept at the art.

Rural grillers and their guests are equipped with a saintly degree of patience that enables them to calmly endure long, leisurely hours while they wait for the hardwood to take light and slowly turn to white-hot coals. Then they continue to wait as the meat roasts slowly on the grill.

Urban grillers, on the other hand, are an impatient breed. These desperate carnivores are willing to wait for nothing. Forget about carefully building fires to transform wood into glowing embers. They break with time-honored tradition, using gas grills or rushing the coals with blowers or hair dryers, or, when technology fails, they resort to huffing and puffing as they take turns blowing on the coals to produce the whitish ash that signals the moment to place the meat on the grill. Of course they choose thinner cuts of meat so they can pull their piece off the grill as soon as possible.

In both cases, the guests longingly watch the process at the grill, distracted, chatting about insignificant matters, heady with the aromas that waft from the grill. The bolder among them approach the fire, inspect its progress with a knowing air and suggest modifications to the distribution of coals or the height of the grill, but when they dare to pick up a knife and attempt to slice off a piece to test its progress, they meet with the firm opposition of the Grill Master. Nobody, not even the best of friends, crosses that line.

A good barbecue cannot be rushed. Hurrying the process, as tends to happen more often in the city than in the country, has a negative effect on the outcome of the grilled meat; it strains the atmosphere and limits the overall enjoyment of the event.

The success of a barbecue depends almost entirely upon the skill of the griller and his (or her) ability to properly plan for, select, prepare, and grill each cut of meat to perfection. This book will guide you through the most important techniques involved in the process of grilling and will reveal the secrets necessary to turn your next barbecue into a truly memorable event.

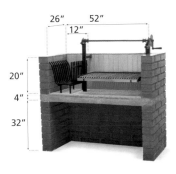

The variety of grills available today is astounding. They come in every shape and size, from very simple to very complex, from traditional charcoal barbecue pits to sophisticated gas grills. The best grill is the one that allows you to manage the temperature and meat easily. Other important considerations include cost and the place and frequency of use. The following are the most common grilling systems used in South America:

BARBECUE PIT: This is the largest and most solid type of grill and the best choice for a definitive installation. The walls of the pit and its 4-inch thick concrete slab base are covered with firebrick. The free space below the base can be used for storing wood and charcoal. A good size is 52 inches wide with a 12-inch space to incorporate a firebox on one side. It stands 36 inches from the ground and its useful measurements are 26 x 52 inches. A system can be devised to raise and lower the grate using a horizontal shaft attached to two steel cables with a crank on one end. A much

more economical option is to manually adjust the height of the grate via metal stops embedded in the wall at three different heights (6, 8, and 10 inches). The grilling surface itself measures 24 x 40 inches and can be made with flat or angled cast iron bars, enameled cast iron, or stainless steel. Enameled cast iron is the most desireable because it won't rust and transmits heat more readily than stainless steel. Grills made with V-shaped angles allow grease to run off into a drip pan.

SKEWER: This is the simplest form of spit and originally consisted of a sharpened wooden rod that pierced the meat lengthwise and was held over the fire. Today skewers are made with stainless steel and may be single or double. The single skewer is used for ribs, cuts of meat, hearts, wings, and onions. The double skewer is used for whole pieces of meat, sausages, and chicken thighs. They should be placed on a 40 x 20 inch grill with at least 3 levels (6, 10, and 14 inches) to hold the skewers. This system has the great advantage of allowing meats that require different cooking times and temperatures to be grilled together. Meats that need higher temperatures and shorter cooking times are placed at lower levels, closest to the coals, while larger cuts, which require longer cooking times, are placed higher up and farther from the heat.

PORTABLE GRILLS: Those with rounded or flat bottoms are the most popular due to their low cost and large surface area for grilling. They usually have a capacity to serve up to 20 people. The round-bottom grill consists of a 50-gallon steel drum cut in half lengthwise. One half is mounted on a four-legged metal frame. The grilling grate is approximately the same size as the edges of the drum (24 x 35 inches) and is raised by four vertical plates welded to the sides of the drum with notches every 2 inches for inserting the corners of the grate. These grills can also be outfitted with a mechanical method for raising the grate via a horizontal shaft attached to two steel cables and with a crank on one end.

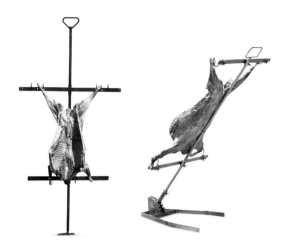

HORIZONTAL AND VERTICAL SPITS: The traditional horizontal spit was little more than a simple wooden shaft sharpened on one end like a skewer onto which the meat is inserted. Today the wooden pole has been replaced by a sharpened metal blade. Two fork-shaped supports are inserted into the ground on either side of the fire, the shaft is laid over the forks, and the skewered meat is turned over the coals, rotisserie style. Another option is the vertical spit made of cast iron or stainless steel with a 5 ½-foot high vertical post and two horizontal crossbars up to 3 feet wide. The meat is attached to the crossbars with hooks adjusted to the size of the beef ribs, lamb, or pig to be grilled. This is clearly the best system for roasting whole animals as the meat cooks slowly and allows the fat to melt and run over the surface of the animal, browning the meat exceptionally well and impregnating it with a uniquely delicious flavor.

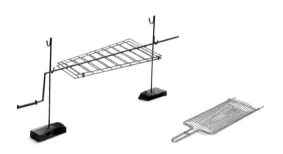

GAS GRILL: These have become popular in large cities, especially for apartment-dwellers whose smaller spaces make it more difficult to light charcoal. Gas grills are a good alternative for grilling faster-cooking meats such as steaks and hamburgers. Gas burners are installed in the back of a rectangular container and a heavy cast iron grate holding volcanic rocks or ceramic briquettes that are heated until they glow like red-hot coals. These grills usually have two grates placed 6 and 12 inches above the briquettes. Their height cannot usually be modified, but the intensity of the heat can be adjusted by regulating the gas supply as on a kitchen stove.

ROTATING FISH GRILL: This is a hinged grilling basket that holds the fish firmly inside. Its shape and size are appropriate for a single large fish, such as a salmon or swordfish. The basket is 30 inches long and 16 inches wide on one end and 10 inches wide on the other. A metal bar is welded lengthwise to one of the grates and rests upon two vertical metal supports anchored in the ground. One end of the bar extends out 8 inches and is shaped into a crank handle so the fish can be turned and roasted over the coals rotisserie style. Another option is the fish basket that rests on top of a regular grill. This allows the fish to be turned easily without breaking apart.

There is an infinite number of tools and utensils on the market today that help the Grill Master in his work: lighting the fire, managing the coals, handling the meat, or cleaning the grill. It is not necessary to have an arsenal of tools to show off one's abilities and skills; strictly speaking, a good knife is the only tool that is absolutely essential.

BUTCHER KNIFE: Choose one with an 8-inch blade, 1 to 2 inches wide, and preferably made of excellent-quality stainless steel. These knives are easy to care for and the edge is very long-lasting, unlike the poor-quality, inexpensive stainless knives available.

SHARPENING STONE: This flat stone made of fine-grained quartz helps keep knife blades sharp. Used with a light mineral oil and the proper technique, your knives will remain in perfect condition for cutting cleanly and easily.

SHARPENING STEEL: A cylindrical bar, ½ inch in diameter with a steel groove, used to maintain a sharp edge on the knives. Don't waste time trying to hone a dull knife with a steel; it won't work. Use a sharpening stone first.

FORK: Use a two-pronged fork with a long handle and a firm structure for lifting heavy pieces of meat and holding grilled meats in place for slicing. Don't use a fork to move meat around while grilling because piercing the meat with the tines will release the juice.

MEAT TONGS: These are used to move meat around on the grill without perforating it. They are best used for relatively light cuts of meat.

CUTTING BOARD: Choose one that is made of heavy wood, 10 x 17 inches and 1 ¼ inch thick with a groove around the outer edge to catch the juices released when the meat is sliced.

APRON: A heavy cotton bib-apron will protect the Grill Master from splashes and spatters. A dark color is best so spots are less noticeable.

LEATHER GLOVES: Protect hands from heat while working with the coals. They are essential when using vertical or horizontal spit grills and will help avoid getting your hands dirty when handling charcoal.

WIRE BRUSH: Used to clean metal grates. Do not use a wire brush on enameled surfaces.

FIREBOX: This is a cast iron basket used to prepare the coals. It's placed to one side of the grill grate or may be built into the wall itself. The broken coals fall to the bottom and are then easily distributed with a poker. The most resistant models are made with ½ inch cast iron bars. The ideal firebox is 20 inches long, 10 inches wide, 12 inches high, and set on 4-inch legs.

SHOVEL OR POKER: Used to distribute the coals under the grill. A shovel with raised sides or an iron poker ¼ inch thick and 28 inches long with a 2 x 4-inch metal plate welded to one side is sufficient.

TERRA-COTTA SERVING DISHES: Keep at least 2 on hand and warm them over the coals just prior to cutting the meat. Use one to serve your guests while the other keeps the remaining meat hot on the grill. Be sure to use a pot holder when handling them to avoid burns.

CHARCOAL AND FIREWOOD

Organic fuels, such as charcoal and hardwood, are preferable for grilling, although natural gas is also acceptable. Do not use petroleum-derived products such as lighter fluid because the strong odor contaminates the grease, which tends to absorb smells.

CHARCOAL: Use charcoal made from hardwoods, such as beech, maple, birch, oak, and hickory, which burn longer than other woods. This is especially important for thick cuts of meat. The belief that natural wood aromas impregnate the meat is erroneous because the wood's aromatic elements are eliminated during the long process of turning it into charcoal. The characteristic roasted aromas are produced by the fat that has melted and gasified during the grilling process.

CHARCOAL QUANTITY AND QUALITY: The amount of charcoal to have on hand is directly related to the time the grill will be in use. If the meat needs anywhere from 90 minutes to 3 hours of cooking time, such as for a Rib Eye, Tip of Bottom Round, or Rack of Ribs, plan on 2 pounds of charcoal for each pound of meat. For meats with shorter cooking times, such as steaks, hamburgers, and sausages, 1 pound of charcoal per pound of meat is sufficient. The Grilling Techniques section provides recommendations on the minimum quantity of charcoal needed for each type of meat. The amount of charcoal on hand should increase in direct proportion to the additional pounds of meat to be grilled.

PREPARING THE COALS: The meat should never be placed on the grill until the coals are "ready." That means that the flames have subsided, the black color of the charcoal has completely disappeared, and the coals are covered with a thin layer of whitish ash. Attempting to rush the process by adding the meat to the grill before the coals are ready leads to inferior results as the meat will be contaminated by the unpleasant flavor of the toxic gases released during combustion.

HARDWOOD: This is the ideal fuel for open-air grilling as it produces excellent coals and a light smoke that adds a very nice touch of flavor to the meat. The woods most commonly used in Patagonia are hawthorn and from fruit trees. Eucalyptus and grape vine cuttings are also commonly used. The amount of time the coals will last depends on the type of wood; the heavier and harder the wood, the longer it will burn.

RECENTLY-LIT CHARCOAL EMITS GASES THAT CAN CONTAMINATE THE MEAT WITH UNPLEASANT FLAVORS. WAIT UNTIL THE COALS ARE "READY" BEFORE ADDING MEAT TO THE GRILL. THE COALS ARE READY WHEN THE FLAMES HAVE SUBSIDED, THE BLACK COLOR OF THE CHARCOAL HAS COMPLETELY DISAPPEARED, AND THE COALS ARE COVERED WITH A THIN LAYER OF WHITISH ASH.

LIGHTING THE FIRE TAKES
TIME, NO MATTER WHICH
TECHNIQUE YOU USE.
PLAN AHEAD TO AVOID
RUSHING OR DELAYS AS
YOUR GUESTS ARRIVE.

LIGHTING CHARCOAL WITH A PAPER CHIMNEY: Loosely wrap a wine bottle with a couple sheets of newspaper up to its neck. Place the wrapped bottle upright in the center of the grilling area and make a cone-shaped mound around it with the charcoal. Do not cover the top of the bottle. Carefully remove the bottle, being careful not to topple the charcoal. Light another piece of newspaper, drop it into the center of the paper chimney, and be patient while the charcoal begins to light.

MAKING COALS WITH A FIREBOX: This is the best system to use for producing coals for grilling. The advantage is that it can produce coals continuously without disturbing the grilling process. Consider a space for this device when designing a barbecue grill. Charcoal is placed in the grill and lit with paper wicks. As the coals burn, they drop into the base of the grill and can be distributed with a poker.

LIGHTING FIREWOOD WITH THE PYRAMID TECHNIQUE: Make 5 'wicks' by lightly twisting sheets of newspaper. Place them in the fireplace and add kindling such as wood chips or dried branches on top. Arrange thin pieces of firewood in a pyramid shape over the kindling and finally add the heavier firewood that will form the coals on top. Be sure not to cover the wicks completely; light one to start the fire. Once coals have formed, distribute them with a shovel beneath the grill or spit, taking care to keep damp or flaming woods at a distance.

MEAT QUALITY

Make friends with your butcher. Find one you can trust to provide you with top-quality meats and who will openly tell you when they aren't. That way you know that you're getting what you pay for. It isn't easy for the inexperienced griller to identify the different cuts of beef, but it only takes a little training for the difference to become clear. The "International Guide to Meats" found on the back flap of this book will help.

BEEF

In theory, any cut of beef can be grilled, but that doesn't mean that all cuts are good cuts. It's something altogether different to choose the right piece of beef for excellent flavor, tenderness, and appearance. The animal's most active muscles are lean and tough and have other culinary uses. The cuts of beef intended for grilling have very specific and easily-identifiable shapes.

Fresh cuts of beef should be bright cherry red with a cream-colored fatty covering; they are well-marbled and look appetizing. The term "marbling" refers to the little dots of fat interspersed throughout the meaty tissue. The more it has, the more tender and flavorful the meat will be. The meat should be elastic and spring back when pressed with a finger. It should also have a mild, fresh-meat aroma; a strong smell indicates that it has been excessively exposed to air and should be avoided.

Plastic-wrapped beef offers no aromatic clues to its freshness, so be sure to check the expiration date carefully. Vacuum-packed meats are not the best choices for outdoor cooking, nor are meats that have been frozen and thawed, because they tend to lose their juices on the grill.

FACTORS OF QUALITY

BREEDS: The best beef for grilling comes from Hereford, Shorthorn, and Aberdeen Angus cattle. These English breeds mature very quickly and therefore form abundant intramuscular fat at an early age. This adds exceptional quality in terms of flavor, tenderness, and juiciness.

BREEDING: The way cattle are raised is a critical factor in the quality of the meat and its marbling. Animals allowed to graze on grassy flatlands and provided with cereal supplements produce meat that is far superior to that of livestock raised on rough terrain that requires them to exert greater physical effort.

AGE: The age of the animal affects the flavor, consistency, and juiciness of its meat. Veal from a young calf is much more tender and juicy than meat from a young bull, although it is less flavorful. As the animal gets older and heavier, its meat becomes more flavorful but loses tenderness and juiciness. Balance is the key for choosing the ideal cut. The best meat for grilling comes from a young bull or heifer 1 to 2 years of age and weighing 650 to 900 pounds.

A "CUT" IS A MUSCLE OR PIECE OF MEAT OBTAINED FROM BUTCHERING THE ANIMAL. A "SIDE OF BEEF" REFERS TO HALF OF A STEER CARCASS THAT IS DRESSED AND READY FOR BUTCHERING.

FOR TENDER AND FLAVORFUL
GRILLED MEATS, LOOK FOR
WELL-MARBLED CUTS. THEY
WILL HAVE LITTLE DOTS OF FAT
INTERSPERSED THROUGHOUT
THE FLESH.

OTHER MEATS

PORK: Ribs are definitely the best cut of pork for grilling. Other choices, such as chops, loin, and tenderloin, should be marinated first; they are too lean for grilling otherwise. The best quality pork meat comes from a suckling pig, which is very tender and juicy.

LAMB: Every cut from a spring lamb weighing no more than 30 pounds is ideal for grilling.

YOUNG GOAT: Choose an animal of no more than 20 pounds with plenty of fat for grilling.

CHICKEN: Look for corn-fed chicken for the best taste.

FISH: Although there are thousands of species of fish, few are recommended for grilling. The flesh should be firm and hold together while cooking and have sufficient fat to balance the possible seasonings. The fish should have thick skin and a solid bone structure so it will hold its shape while grilling. Popular choices in Patagonia are Salmon, Grouper, Sierra, Dorado, Mackerel, Reineta, and on special occasions, Trout. When buying fish, be sure that the gills are bright red and moist. The eyes should be bright and shiny and the meat firm; it should spring back when pressed with a finger and not leave an indentation. The smell should be mild and pleasant.

MATURATION: This is the natural process that the animal's musculature undergoes after slaughter. The meat remains elastic for the first few hours, but as it cools rigor mortis sets in and lasts for approximately 6 hours. This post-mortem rigidity may be a bit shorter if the room temperature is relatively high. Once the muscles relax again, a slow process of muscular lysis (cell break-down) begins as a result of proteolytic enzymes that reach their peak at 6 days in a cold environment.

FAT: In grilling, fat is essential for flavor, juiciness, and "that special touch." The meat's fat covering melts with the heat, drips over the coals, gasifies, and permeates the meat with its aroma. The residual fat that doesn't melt browns and helps toast the surface proteins. The fat marbled throughout the meat also heightens the flavor for a taste that is impossible to achieve with lean meats.

FAT DEPOSITS ON THE INSIDE
OF LAMB AND GOATS SHOULD BE
VISIBLE BUT NOT EXCESSIVE,
AS IN THE PHOTO. WHEN
THERE IS TOO LITTLE FAT, THE
GRILLED MEAT WILL BE DRY
AND TOUGH; IF THERE IS TOO
MUCH, IT WILL HAVE
AN OVERLY-STRONG FLAVOR
AND AROMA.

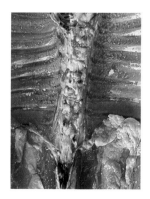

TIPS AND TECHNIQUES

The tips and techniques presented here will help maximize the aroma, flavor, and appearance of your barbecue.

GRILLING TO PERFECTION

Whatever the type of meat, grilling technique, or griller's personal style, there are 3 key conditions for perfectly-grilled meat:

1. Juice retention: When the meat has been cut into pieces or when the protective membranes have been removed and the muscular fibers exposed, the meat should be seared first to seal in the juices. The meat is briefly exposed to very high heat (325° to 400°F) to coagulate, dehydrate, and toast the surface proteins and produce a nicely browned seal. This is not necessary when grilling a whole piece of meat as its encapsulating membranes and peripheral fat layer will naturally protect it from fluid loss.

2. The right temperature: Cook the meat at a temperature that is proportionally inverse to its size and thickness; the bigger and thicker the piece of meat, the lower the heat should be. Conversely, smaller, thinner cuts should be cooked over higher heat.

3. Perfect timing: Cooking time should be directly proportional to the meat's size and thickness; the thinner the piece of meat, the shorter the cooking time should be. Conversely, bigger and thicker cuts should have longer cooking times.

MANAGING GRILL TEMPERATURE

Temperature management is one of the Grill Master's primary responsibilities; the quality of the grilling process depends on it. This becomes increasingly important as the size and thickness of the meat increases, particularly with cuts such as Rib Eye, Short Plate, Ribs, and whole animals.

CONCENTRATING THE COALS UNDER THE MEAT: The amount of heat that reaches the different cuts of meat can be controlled through the concentration of the coals under the grilling grate. Distribute the coals with a poker according to the intensity of the heat needed. To ensure uniform cooking, the perimeter of the coal layer should extend at least 2 inches beyond that of the meat.

DISTANCE BETWEEN THE MEAT AND THE COALS: Once the coals have been distributed, the grilling technique used will determine the distance between the meat and the coals. If the meat needs to be sealed, it should be positioned closer to the coals to receive the initial high heat necessary for searing. The grate will later be raised for a more moderate cooking temperature.

KEEPING THE COALS GLOWING: Depending on the quality of the charcoal used, the initial batch of coals will burn evenly for 30 to 60 minutes. The cooking temperature can be regulated by adjusting the distance between the meat and the coals. As the embers begin to die down, the Grill Master should move the meat lower or replace the older coals with new ones in order to maintain the proper temperature until grilling is completed. When the projected cooking time dictates that additional coals will be needed, prepare them separately on another fire or in a corner of the grill away from the meat.

EVERY GRILLER AIMS FOR THE HIGHEST DEGREE OF QUALITY. THE PEAK IS REACHED WHEN THE MEAT HAS SIMULTANEOUSLY OBTAINED THE MAXIMUM DEGREE OF JUICINESS WITH A BRIGHT REDDISH CENTER AND A WELL-BROWNED OUTER SURFACE.

MANAGING THE TEMPERATURE OF SPIT GRILLS

Temperature management requires a different technique for a vertical spit than it does for a regular grill as the meat is cooked with the indirect heat that radiates from the fire. The spit is placed at a distance from the fire that allows the meat to receive part of the radiation of the flames while avoiding the smoke from the combustion of the wood. The temperature is managed by varying the distance between the spit and the fire, the speed with which wood is added to the fire, and the inclination and position of the spit. The spit should never be left unattended as changes in wind can alter the cooking temperature.

ESTIMATING THE TEMPERATURE

A simple method for estimating the cooking temperature is to hold the palm of your hand over the coals at the same height as the meat and count the seconds that you can resist the heat.

1-2 SECONDS: High heat (350 to 400ºF), used to sear the meat to seal in juices. The surface of the meat will burn if this temperature is maintained more than 10 minutes.

3-4 SECONDS: Medium high heat (250 to 350ºF), used for thin cuts and steaks.

5-6 SECONDS: Medium heat (200 to 250ºF), used for roasting thick cuts and whole animals on vertical spits. This temperature should be maintained throughout the entire cooking process.

SEALING THE MEAT

It is important to seal in the juices of smaller cuts of meat and those without a protective membrane. This is done by briefly searing the meat over very high heat, which coagulates and toasts the proteins and caramelizes the sugars on its surface.

To ensure that the meat is evenly sealed, the hot coals should be distributed so that the same temperature (350 to 400ºF) reaches all parts of the meat evenly. The intense initial burst of heat will later be reduced to allow the meat to cook more slowly and the interior to reach the desired degree of doneness without burning the outside.

It is advisable to seal all cuts that do not have membranes or a layer of fat, such as Rib Eye and Strip Loin. Steaks should be browned even more intensely than larger cuts because they will spend less time on the grill.

ONCE THE COALS ARE READY THEY ARE ARRANGED UNDER THE GRILLING GRATE. FOR PROPER HEAT DISTRIBUTION, THE COALS SHOULD EXTEND AT LEAST 2 INCHES BEYOND THE SURFACE THAT THE MEAT WILL OCCUPY ON THE GRILL.

TO ESTIMATE THE TEMPERATURE THAT REACHES THE MEAT, HOLD THE PALM OF YOUR HAND OVER THE COALS AT THE SAME HEIGHT AS THE MEAT AND COUNT THE SECONDS THAT YOU CAN TOLERATE THE HEAT. A MEDIUM TEMPERATURE IS 5 TO 6 SECONDS.

GRILLING PROCESS

During grilling, the surface of the meat receives heat through the radiation of the coals and flames and the convection of hot air; the interior of the meat cooks as the heat moves inward toward the center of the grilled cut.

As the heat penetrates the meat, the muscle fibers contract and the liquids contained in them move outward toward the spaces between the fibers. This liquid, or "juice," increases as the muscle fibers retract until the exterior barrier of the meat can no longer prevent the liquids from leaking outward and progressive dehydration begins.

SALTING THE MEAT

The decision to salt the meat depends on whether or not it is protected by membranes or a layer of fat. Salt is very hygroscopic, which means that it strongly attracts moisture; it absorbs water and dissolves into it.

Sprinkling salt over the surface of the meat draws its interior liquids out to the surface. As the salt dissolves, it penetrates the protective membranes by osmosis,

slowly mixes with the intercellular liquids, and deeply seasons the meat.

This transference of salt through osmosis from the surface of the meat to its interior only takes place with whole cuts that have their membranes intact. Salt works differently with meat that has been cut because it draws the juices to the surface, which moistens the meat and prevents it from forming a seal.

When the meat is placed on the grill, the heat causes the muscle fibers to contract, placing pressure on the intercellular liquids. When the meat has not been properly sealed or has no natural membrane barrier, the juices flow out to the surface and coagulate there. This not only looks unattractive, but it also prevents the meat from browning, which in turn causes it to dry out.

Many people believe that it is best to use coarse salt when grilling, although in fact, the type of salt used, fine or coarse, is not a significant factor for quality. Fine salt applied in the right quantity penetrates rapidly and seasons the meat more uniformly than coarse salt. It also has the added benefit of not leaving unpleasant salty residues on the meat. Use whichever type of salt you prefer, as both have the same affect.

WHEN TO SALT

Salt should be applied ahead of time to whole animals and meat with its protective membranes intact. Lamb and any other animal to be roasted whole should be salted at least 2 hours before grilling. Steaks, butcher's cuts, and thawed meats should only be salted after they have been seared and the juices sealed in. For very thin cuts, such as Skirt Steak, wait to add salt until after it has been grilled.

THE BIGGER THE PIECE OF MEAT, THE EARLIER THE SALT SHOULD BE APPLIED. SALT WELL-BROWNED SECTIONS OF THIN CUTS AND STEAKS AFTER SEARING.

HOW TO SHARPEN A KNIFE

To maintain a sharp edge on a knife it is necessary to have a sharpening stone, ideally two-sided: one fine-grained, the other medium-grained. Moisten the stone with light mineral oil and place the part of the blade closest to the handle on the stone at a 20° angle and slide it in a circular motion first clockwise on one side, then counterclockwise on the other side. Using a smaller angle to the stone will produce a sharper edge.

HOW AND WHEN TO CARVE

Knowing just the right moment to take the meat off the grill and begin carving it at its peak of perfection is the only secret you'll have to discover for yourself. Mastering this art requires the experience gained with countless hours at the grill over the course of a lifetime. When the meat is cooked just right, take it off the grill or spit and wait a few minutes for its juices to settle. Then carve and serve it quickly.

FOR RIBS: Place the ribs face up and slice between them.

FOR WHOLE ANIMALS: An experienced Grill Master can carve an entire lamb, kid, or suckling pig in just 3 minutes. Work more slowly and the meat will cool and lose its juiciness. Begin by separating the shoulders and legs, and then carve slices of meat with the knife. Keep a warm clay serving dish on hand to hold the pieces of meat. When it is relatively full, ask an assistant to begin serving the guests, and continue on with the ribs. Use a meat cleaver to split the backbone in two and then separate the ribs with a knife. It is recommendable to have another clay dish on hand to receive the meat as you carve.

FREEZING AND THAWING

Freezing meat at 0°F allows for long-time preservation, although it is advisable to use it within 6 months because the cellular structure deteriorates due to the effect of the crystallization of its aqueous components. The ice crystals rupture the cell membranes and allow the juices to flow to the exterior of the thawed meat, making it less desirable for grilling. Whenever frozen meat is to be used, thaw it slowly by transferring it from the freezer to the refrigerator 24 to 48 hours before use.

Never use frozen fish for grilling! Its fragile muscular structure is unable to withstand the heat of the grill and its oils tend to oxidize, giving it a very unpleasant, rancid flavor.

COLD AGING MEATS

Holding meat at low temperatures slows the onset of the fermentation and decomposition processes, but it simultaneously encourages the "ripening" process, which tenderizes the meat and intensifies the flavor. Meat can be aged in the refrigerator at 40°F for 4 or 5 days, although longer periods are not recommended; most home refrigerators do not maintain temperatures that are low enough – and stable enough – to prevent decomposition.

For best results with beef, remove it at least a couple hours before cooking because abrupt changes in temperature can harden the meat.

Ducks and chickens can be held in the refrigerator for 1 or 2 days, but should be removed from their commercial plastic wrap, washed, and dried well before storing. Fresh fish should not be held more than 24 hours in the refrigerator: the sooner they are grilled the better!

CARVE AND SERVE GRILLED MEATS QUICKLY SO THEY DON'T GET COLD. HAVE ALL YOUR EQUIPMENT READY AND AT HAND, INCLUDING A STURDY TABLE, A LARGE CUTTING BOARD, A SHARP KNIFE, A HEAVY MEAT CLEAVER, A FORK, AND PRE-WARMED SERVING DISHES.

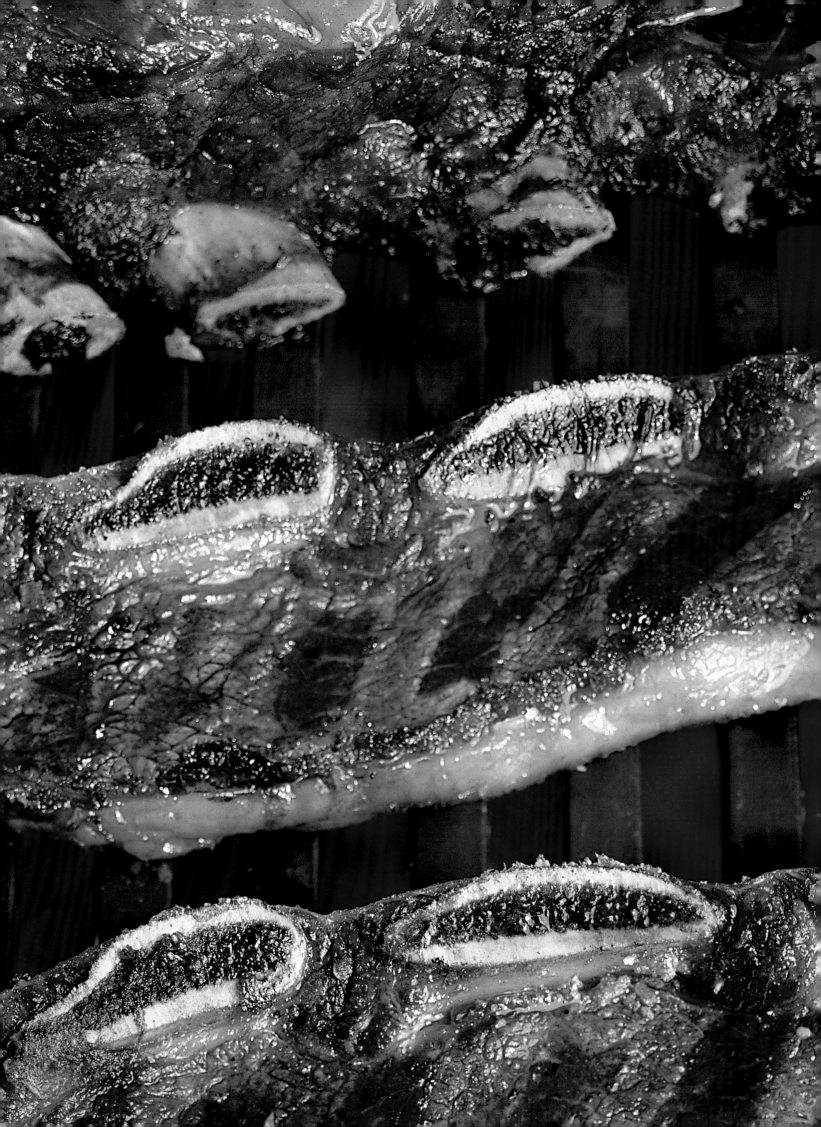

BEEF

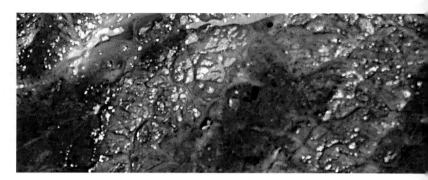

Back Ribs

Costillar

This is the flattest part of the beef ribs. The meat is well marbled and the outside is covered with a thick layer of fat that browns and then melts slowly with the heat, infusing the meat – and the air – with a delicious aroma. The combination of the fat and bone marrow lend the ribs an extraordinary flavor. Slow grilling results in tender, juicy meat that is without a doubt the most flavorful of any cut of beef.

Technical Information

WEIGHT: *15 to 18 lbs*
SERVES: *7 to 8 people*
TIME: *3 hours*
HEAT: *medium*
HARDWOOD: *65 lbs minimum*
CHARCOAL: *25 lbs minimum*

Grilling Techniques

1 Ask the butcher to cut the ribs crosswise (perpendicular) with a saw. It is important that he cut only the ribs and not the meat to prevent it from losing its ability to retain juices. At least two cuts should be made so that the rack of ribs can be divided into 3 lengthwise portions.
2 Salt both sides 1 hour before grilling.

ON A VERTICAL SPIT

1 Attach the hooks of the crossbars between the ribs. The crossbars should attach to the outer side, leaving the ribs open to maximum exposure to the heat.
2 Place the vertical spit with the ribs facing the fire (meaty side out) and at a distance that provides a medium temperature. Roast for 2 hours on that side. The marrow and the fat will melt and permeate the meat.
3 When the ribs are well-browned, turn the spit 180° and grill for another hour or until the layer of fat has browned and reduced. The temperature should be a little lower than it was in step 2 because fat burns more easily.

ON THE GRILL

1 Place the ribs over the coals at medium heat for 2 hours. The meat will cook slowly with the heat from the grill aided by the warmth conducted through the bones, which further infuses the meat with the flavor of the bone marrow.
2 When the first side is done, the fat on the other side should feel warm. Turn them over and grill another 30 minutes or until golden.

SECRET
BE PATIENT WITH THIS MEAT.
IT NEEDS SLOW, CAREFUL
GRILLING TO BRING OUT ITS BEST
CHARACTERISTICS.

Rib Eye
Bife Ancho or Lomo Vetado

This is a thick, rectangular-shaped cut with good intramuscular marbling that contributes excellent flavor. It consists of a central muscle called the "Eye of the Loin" and other half-moon-shaped peripheral muscles. The "Eye" is similar in consistency to Short Loin, but it has a richer flavor due to the peripheral muscles that are highly saturated with fats that permeate the meat as it cooks. This is a very fine cut and is usually delicious when grilled. Although the Rib Eye is best roasted whole, it can also be grilled as 1 ½-inch thick steaks, following the technique suggested in Top Loin Steak. Wrap a string around the perimeter of the steak once or twice to prevent the peripheral muscles from pulling away from the eye and losing the juicy flavor through the cracks.

Technical Information

WEIGHT: 5 ½ to 8 lbs

SERVES: 6 to 9 people

TIME: 2 hours 30 min

HEAT: medium

CHARCOAL: 13 lbs minimum

Grilling Technique

1 Quickly sear both sides of the Rib Eye over high heat to seal in its juices; 5 minutes per side.

2 Add salt after it has been sealed and lower the temperature to medium.

3 Place fatty side down over the coals and grill for 1 hour and 15 minutes.

4 When pink drops appear on the upper side, turn the meat over and continue to cook over medium heat for another hour.

Tip of Bottom Round
Tapa de Cuadril or Punta de Ganso

This is the favorite cut for grilling in Brazil, where it is known as Picanha. It is the pyramid-shaped end of the muscle where the round, rump, and sirloin come together. The closer the portion is to the apex of the pyramid, the more tender and juicy it will be. One side is covered by a layer of fat that is the key to its magnificent flavor. This is a delicious cut that works very well on the grill as long as the fat layer is conserved. It is tender and juicy with a buttery aroma.

Technical Information

WEIGHT: 4 ½ to 5 ½ lbs
SERVES: 5 to 7 people
TIME: 2 hours
HEAT: medium
CHARCOAL: 15 lbs minimum

Grilling Technique

1 Cook, fatty side down, over the coals for 1 ½ hours. The fat will brown and slowly melt down to a thin layer. This process lends this cut its unique buttery flavor and aroma.

2 When drops of juice appear on the upper side, add salt, turn it over, and let it cook over medium heat for 30 minutes longer, until the lean side is nicely browned.

3 Before removing the meat from the grill, turn it over and reheat the fatty side over high heat for 3 minutes. The toasted fat should be hot when it reaches the table.

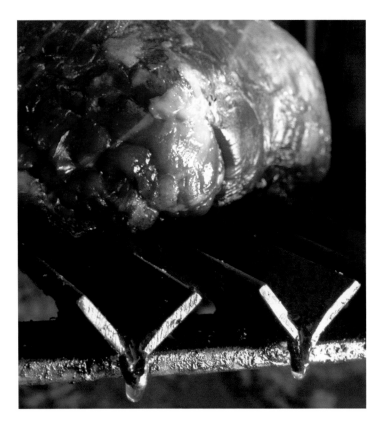

SECRET

THE LAYER OF FAT IS ESSENTIAL IN THIS CUT. ONLY BUY PIECES THAT HAVE THIS LAYER INTACT.

FAT MELTING ONTO THE COALS CAN CAUSE FLARE-UPS THAT SHOULD BE PUT OUT IMMEDIATELY BY SPREADING A LAYER OF COLD ASHES OVER THE FLAMES OR SPRINKLING SOME WATER ON THEM.

Flap
Centro de Vacío or Tapabarriga

This is a thick, triangular cut formed by three muscles that cover the abdominal wall. The two smaller muscles cover the main muscle, or "Flap," which we've used for this Grilling Technique. This is a flavorful and tender cut of meat when it comes from a young animal. It contracts tightly when grilled and takes on the shape of a Tenderloin. The smaller muscles have a firm texture and are less suitable for grilling. Leave the membrane and fat intact to maintain its juiciness.

Technical Information

WEIGHT: *3 ½ to 4 ½ lbs*

SERVES: *4 to 5 people*

TIME: *1 hour*

HEAT: *medium*

CHARCOAL: *7 lbs minimum*

Grilling Technique

1 Carefully separate the Flap's center muscle, being careful to conserve the fine membrane that encloses it.

2 Sear it over high heat, 5 minutes per side, to seal in the juices.

3 Add salt after searing and lower the temperature to medium heat. Grill for 30 minutes.

4 When pinkish drops appear on the thickest part of the meat, turn it over and cook for another 20 minutes.

SECRET

ONLY USE FLAP FROM A YOUNG
ANIMAL TO ENSURE A TENDER CUT.

Short Plate
Tapa de Asado or Plateada

This medium thick cut has an irregular rectangular flat shape. The outer side is covered with nearly ½ inch of fat. Once browned and slowly reduced, this fat contributes a unique flavor. The meat is quite firm and can sometimes be tough if it it comes from an older animal. Grill it slowly for a flavorful and moderately juicy roast.

Technical Information

WEIGHT: *5 ½ to 7 lbs*
SERVES: *6 to 8 people*
TIME: *2 hours 30 min*
HEAT: *medium*
CHARCOAL: *13 lbs minimum*

Grilling Technique

1 Sprinkle salt on both sides of the meat before grilling.
2 Place the meat fatty side down on the grill over medium heat for 2 hours. The objective of this first stage is to allow the fat to brown and reduce slowly until it becomes a crisp, thin layer. Control the intensity of the fire constantly and be careful not to let the fat burn.
3 Turn the meat over and grill over medium heat for 30 minutes or until nicely browned.
4 Slice against the grain and serve quickly because this cut toughens as it cools.

SECRET
THE FAT LAYER IS ESSENTIAL IN THE SHORT PLATE. THIS MEAT IS WORTHLESS FOR GRILLING WITHOUT THE FAT. ONLY BUY PIECES WITH THE FAT LEFT INTACT.

Tenderloin
Lomo or Filete

Thick and round on one end and flat on the other, the Tenderloin is a cylindrical muscle with very little fat or marbling. It is considered the tenderest cut of beef, and, due to its proximity to the intra-abdominal viscera, it has a very delicate flavor that is different from other cuts closer to the outer surface of the animal. Its scant marbling makes it recommendable for people on low-fat diets.

Technical Information

WEIGHT: *5 ½ lb to 8 lb*

SERVES: *6 to 9 people*

TIME: *1 hr 10 min*

HEAT: *medium*

CHARCOAL: *9 lbs minimum*

Grilling Techniques

FULL CUT

1 Sear both sides over high heat, 5 minutes per side, to seal in the juices.
2 Add salt to both sides after searing, lower the temperature to medium heat, and grill for 30 minutes.
3 When pinkish drops appear on the upper side, turn the meat over and cook for another 30 minutes.

STEAKS

1 Cut the Tenderloin into individual steaks 1 ½ to 2 inches thick. Tie each with butcher's string to conserve the round shape during grilling.
2 Sear both sides over high heat, 5 minutes per side, to seal in the juices.
3 Add salt after searing, adjust the temperature to medium-high, and grill 8 minutes per side or until browned.

SECRET

TENDERLOIN COOKS VERY QUICKLY AND CAN TURN FROM JUICY AND TENDER TO DRY AND TOUGH IN A MATTER OF MINUTES. DO NOT OVERCOOK.

Tri-Tip

Colita de Cuadril or Punta de Picana

This is a cone-shaped cut with a partial fat covering that adds a unique buttery aroma and flavor. The Tri-Tip is medium-textured and has an excellent flavor. Time and temperature must be watched very carefully while grilling because it goes from rare to well-done very quickly.

Technical Information

WEIGHT: *2 ½ to 3 ½ lbs*
SERVES: *3 to 4 people*
TIME: *1 hour 30 min*
HEAT: *medium*
CHARCOAL: *9 lbs minimum*

Grilling Technique

1 Use this cut for grilling only when it conserves its fat layer. Remove only the fat that extends beyond the edges of the meat.

2 Add salt to the entire surface 1 hour in advance.

3 Place the meat fat-side down over the coals for 50 minutes. The fat will brown, melt slowly, and reduce to a thin layer. This process gives the Tri-Tip its distinctive buttery flavor and aroma.

4 When beads of juice appear on the upper side, turn the meat over and continue grilling over medium heat for 25 minutes longer.

SECRET

THE TRI-TIP'S FAT LAYER IS ESSENTIAL; ONLY BUY IT WITH THE FAT LAYER INTACT. NOTE THAT THE SIDES STILL APPEAR PINK ONCE THE GRILLING TIME IS COMPLETED. DON'T BE FOOLED BY APPEARANCES; THE MEAT REALLY IS COOKED THROUGH.

Short Ribs
Asado de Tira

Short Ribs are strips of ribs with substantial fat content and bone marrow that lend them their extraordinary flavor. Look for Short Ribs from young Angus or Hereford bulls to ensure tender meat. They can be grilled in thin or thick cuts; either way the yield will be low, so calculate at least 1 ½ pounds per person.

Technical Information

SHORT RIBS (THIN)
WIDTH: ½ to 1 inch
WEIGHT: ¾ pound
SERVES: 2 per person
TIME: 15 min
HEAT: high
CHARCOAL: 5 lbs minimum

SHORT RIBS (THICK)
WIDTH: 2 ½ to 4 inches
WEIGHT: 1 ⅓ to 3 ⅓ pounds
SERVES: 1 to 2 people
TIME: 1 hoursr 15 min
HEAT: medium
CHARCOAL: 9 lbs minimum

Grilling Techniques

SHORT RIBS (THIN CUT)

1 Sear both sides over high heat, 5 minutes per side, to seal in the juices. Continue grilling a few minutes longer until they are nicely browned on both sides.

2 Apply salt on each side after browning.

SHORT RIBS (THICK CUT)

1 Place the meat over the coals, bone side down, and grill for 1 hour over medium heat. Add salt to the fat on the upper side.

2 As the end of the hour approaches, the meat will loosen itself from the bones somewhat and a bit of foam will appear on the marrow of the ribs. Turn the rack over, fat side down, and grill 15 minutes longer or until nicely browned.

SECRET
SERVE THE GRILLED MEAT QUICKLY
BECAUSE IT TOUGHENS AS IT COOLS.

Skirt Steak

This very thin cut comes from the muscles that surround the diaphragm. It is somewhat rounded and may be up to 20 inches long, approximately 2 ½ inches wide, and ½ inch thick. Its location near the abdominal viscera on one side and the thorax on the other lend it a very nice flavor. Both sides are covered with a thick membrane that is usually removed before grilling, although it may be left in place to help conserve the juices during cooking.

Technical Information

WEIGHT: ½ to 1 lb
SERVES: 2 to 3 people
TIME: 30 min
HEAT: medium
CHARCOAL: 5 lbs

Grilling Technique

1 Given the extreme thinness of this cut, place the meat over medium-high heat for just 15 minutes per side. Add salt after browning.
2 Cut the Skirt Steak into ½ inch pieces for snacking while waiting for other cuts of meat to finish cooking.

SECRET
SKIRT STEAK IS A GOOD CHOICE
FOR SNACKING WHILE WAITING
FOR OTHER CUTS OF MEAT
TO FINISH COOKING.

SECRETS OF
THE PATAGONIAN
BARBECUE

Matambre

A true "Matambre" is an irregular square-shaped subcutaneous muscle located just below the skin and above the lower part of the ribs. This thin cut is covered by a thin layer of fat. Flank steak is a suitable substitute. Matambre demands complete concentration on the grill; it must be cooked quickly over high heat or it will become tough and unappetizing. It's perfect for guests to snack on before launching into the rest of the barbecue.

Technical Information

WEIGHT: *2 ¾ to 3 ½ lbs*

SERVES: *3 to 4 people*

TIME: *15 to 20 min*

HEAT: *high*

CHARCOAL: *6 lbs minimum*

Grilling Technique

1 Place the meat on the grill, fatty side down, over high heat for 10 minutes.
2 When the layer of fat has browned and the upper surface begins to exude tiny pink drops, turn the meat over and grill just a few minutes longer.

SECRET

DO NOT REMOVE THE LAYER OF FAT THAT COVERS THE MATAMBRE UNDER ANY CIRCUMSTANCES AS IT PROTECTS THIS THIN MEAT DURING COOKING.

ONLY USE THIS CUT FOR GRILLING WHEN YOU CAN BE SURE THAT IT COMES FROM A YOUNG BULL OR HEIFER.

Flank Steak
Bife de Vacío or Palanca

This thin, lean cut has a medium-firm consistency. Flank and Flap constitute the lateral wall of the animal's abdomen. This meat is very good for snacking while waiting for thicker cuts to grill. It has a very mild flavor that does not compete with other meats.

Technical Information

WEIGHT: *1 ¾ to 2 ¼ lbs*

SERVES: *2 people*

TIME: *40 min*

HEAT: *medium-high*

CHARCOAL: *5 lbs minimum*

Grilling Technique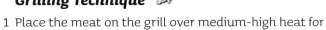

1 Place the meat on the grill over medium-high heat for 15 minutes per side or until nicely browned.
2 Add salt after browning.

SECRET
TO SERVE FLANK STEAK AS PART OF A MEAL, CUT IT ACROSS THE GRAIN IN 1 ¼ INCH-WIDE SLICES, OR OFFER IT AS A SNACK IN BITE-SIZED PIECES.

Strip Loin Steak

Bife de Chorizo

Strip Loin Steak is by far the most popular steak for grilling. It is cut from the Strip Loin and has unbeatable characteristics for grilling. Long, thick, and rectangular, it is covered with a ½-inch layer of fat on all sides for nice, tender steaks with excellent flavor and appearance. A full Boneless Strip Loin weighs 11 to 13 pounds and yields 12 to 15 fourteen-ounce steaks.

Technical Information

THICKNESS: 1 ¼ inches

WEIGHT: 14 to 17 ounces

SERVES: 1 person

TIME: 30 min

HEAT: medium-high

CHARCOAL: 5 lbs minumum

Grilling Technique

1 Sear both sides over high heat, 5 minutes per side, to seal in the juices, and then add salt.

2 Reduce heat to medium-high and continue grilling 10 minutes more per side or until both sides are nicely browned. Use tongs to turn the meat and never pierce it with a fork or knife.

3 Remove the steaks from the grill and serve one per person on warmed plates. If the steaks have been grilled to different degrees of doneness, serve them yourself to avoid confusion.

Rib Steak

Bife con Costilla

A Rib Steak is a 1 ¼ to 1 ½-inch transversal cut of Strip Loin with a piece of rib bone attached. It is often called a "Prime Rib," although strictly speaking, the adjective "Prime" has no direct relationship with quality.

Technical Information

THICKNESS: *1 ¼ to 2 inches*

WEIGHT: *25 ounces*

SERVES: *1 person*

TIME: *30 to 40 min*

HEAT: *medium-high*

CHARCOAL: *5 lbs minimum*

Grilling Technique

1 Sear 5 minutes per side over high heat to seal in the juices, and then add salt.

2 Continue grilling over medium-high heat for 15 to 20 minutes per side until nicely browned. Use tongs to turn the meat; never pierce the meat with a fork or knife.

3 Remove the steaks from the grill and serve them whole on warmed plates, one per person. If the steaks have been grilled to different degrees of doneness, serve them yourself to avoid confusion.

SECRET

THE KEY TO OBTAINING STEAKS THAT ARE BOTH NICELY BROWNED AND JUICY IS TO GRILL AT HIGH TEMPERATURES. THIS IS THE ONLY WAY TO ENSURE THAT THE COOKING AND BROWNING TIMES ARE IN BALANCE.

T-Bone Steak

Bife Angosto con Lomo or Entrecot

The T-bone is a special steak that comes from a 1 ½-inch transversal cut from the Strip Loin. This is the combination of two steaks in one, the Sirloin and the Tenderloin, each with its own texture and flavor. The bone marrow provides an additional infusion of flavor as well.

Technical Information

THICKNESS: 1 ¼ to 1 ½ inches

WEIGHT: 27 ounces

SERVES: 1 person

TIME: 30 to 40 min

HEAT: medium-high

CHARCOAL: 5 lbs minimum

Grilling Technique

1 Sear 5 minutes per side over high heat to seal in the juices. Add salt after sealing.

2 Continue grilling 15 to 20 minutes per side until both are nicely browned. Use tongs to turn the meat; never pierce the meat with a fork or knife.

3 Remove the steaks from the grill and serve them whole on warmed plates, one per person. If the steaks have been grilled to different degrees of doneness, serve them yourself to avoid confusion.

SECRET
THE KEY TO KNOWING THE PRECISE
MOMENT TO TURN THE T-BONE OVER
OR REMOVE IT FROM THE GRILL IS
OBSERVING THE DROPS OF JUICE
THAT FORM ON THE SURFACE.

Variety Meats
Achuras or Interiores

Known as sweetbreads, viscera, offal, or variety meats, these special products provide a wide range of flavors and textures that are very different from those offered by muscle cuts. Sweetbreads refers to two related glands: the thymus gland near the aorta and the thyroid gland in the throat. They make a nice snack for 1 or 2 people.

Kidneys are large lobed organs that are sliced into rounds before grilling. They serve 2 to 3 people as a snack.

Braided Beef Intestines refer to the small intestine braided into a 4-foot chain that reduces by half when cooked. It serves 2 to 3 people as a snack.

Technical Information

TIME: 30 - 45 min
HEAT: medium-high
CHARCOAL: 6 ½ lbs

Grilling Techniques

1 Prepare the individual variety meats for grillling according to the specific instructions listed below.
2 All should be browned on both sides over medium-high heat for about 30 minutes.
3 Use tongs to move them around the grill, and add salt after they are nicely browned.

SWEETBREADS
When sweetbreads come from a young animal they are tender and can be placed directly on the grill without previous cooking, although boiling them in salted water for 5 minutes will prevent them from falling apart.

KIDNEYS
To reduce the strong taste, rinse the kidneys well in several changes of cold water, and then soak them in cold salted water with a couple teaspoons of vinegar for 2 hours. Thread them onto skewers for ease of handling on the grill. Brush them with melted butter while grilling and then dust them with black pepper.

BRAIDED BEEF INTESTINES
The intestines should be boiled in salted water for at least 1 ½ hours before grilling. Allow them to cool in their cooking liquid and then use your fingers to eliminate any peripheral fat. Brown them on the grill, cut them into bite-sized portions, and serve hot.

SECRET
VARIETY MEATS SHOULD ALWAYS BE SERVED COOKED AND HOT. OFFER THEM IN A PRE-HEATED CLAY SERVING DISH TO CONSERVE THEIR TEMPERATURE.

Hamburgers
Hamburguesas

The hamburger's international expansion began when German immigrants came to the United States in the late 19th century and the now-popular sandwich was incorporated into the rural Midwestern diet. Fast food restaurants in the 20th century spread this sandwich throughout the world. The original hamburger was large, the size of a tennis ball, and had enough fat to ensure that it was both juicy and tender. Fast food restaurants reduced their size and increased the amount of fat, privileging speed and low production cost over quality.

Technical Information

WEIGHT: 7 to 9 ounces
SERVES: 1 per person
TIME: 10 to 15 min
HEAT: medium-high
CHARCOAL: 5 lbs minimum

Ingredients

2 ¼ lbs ground beef, 15-18% fat
2 eggs
½ cup bread crumbs
1 onion, finely chopped
½ cup parsley, chopped
Salt and pepper

Grilling Technique

1 Use your hands to mix the ground beef, eggs, and bread crumbs in a bowl. Add the parsley, salt and pepper to taste.
2 Fry the onion until it is well browned and add it to the reserved mixture.
3 To make the hamburger patties, take a bit of the mixture the size of a tennis ball and gently shape it into a patty. Repeat until all the patties are ready.
4 Place the hamburger patties on the grill over medium-high heat for 5 to 7 minutes per side or until nicely browned. Use a metal spatula to turn them over.

Shish-kebobs

Brochetas or Anticuchos

SECRET

PLACE THE INGREDIENTS CLOSELY TOGETHER ON THE SKEWER SO THAT THEIR FLAVORS BLEND WELL. BE SURE TO ADD PLENTY OF MARINADE.

Called "Brochetas" in Argentina and "Anticuchos" in Chile, these bite-sized skewered morsels are always a treat. Beef is used here, but feel free to use other meats or poultry. We don't recommend bacon or sausage, however, because of their overpowering flavor.

Technical Information

SERVES: 1 per person

TIME: 30 min

HEAT: medium-high

CHARCOAL: 5 lbs minimum

Ingredients

2 ¼ lbs Tenderloin Tips or
    Sirloin cubes

2 onions

2 red or green bell peppers

1 tablespoon hot sauce

2 cloves of garlic, crushed

2 tablespoons vinegar

3 tablespoons oil

2 teaspoons black pepper

1 teaspoon cumin

1 ½ teaspoons salt

Grilling Technique

1 Cut the meat into 1 ¼-inch cubes and marinate for 2 hours in a mixture of garlic, oil, vinegar, black pepper, hot sauce, cumin, and salt.

2 Thread the skewers with alternating cubes of meat, onion, and bell peppers.

3 Place the skewers on the grill, leaving the wooden handles well away from the heat so they don't burn. Turn them and brush with more marinade. Remove from the grill when they are well browned and the onion is toasted around the edges. Serve one skewer per person.

PORK

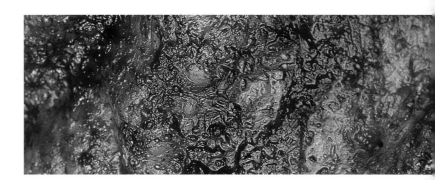

Spit-Roasted Suckling Pig
Lechón al Asador Vertical

There is no other mammal on Earth that can convert its food into meat and fat as completely and competently as the pig. Its very efficient natural metabolism has been further enhanced by genetics, giving rise to new breeds with greater muscular mass and less fat. Butchered at 20 to 65 pounds, a suckling pig has a perfect balance of tenderness and flavor in every one of its cuts. Even its skin enters into this magnificent gastronomic feast when grilled to a crunchy, golden delight.

SECRET

IN ORDER TO FULLY APPRECIATE THE DELICATE FLAVOR OF THE SUCKLING PIG, AVOID USING MARINADES AND SEASONINGS. IF THIS IS YOUR FIRST SPIT-ROASTED SUCKLING PIG, IT'S SURE TO BE THE BEST MEAT YOU'VE EVER TASTED!

Technical Information

WEIGHT: 18 to 35 lbs
SERVES: 8 to 16 people
TIME: 4 to 5 hours
HARDWOOD: 90 lbs minimum

Grilling Technique

1 To prepare the suckling pig for flattening and attaching to a vertical spit: Place the pig on its back on a sturdy table. Open its chest with a cleaver or saw and cut out the breastbone to free the rib cage. Create a hinge effect by making a partial cut through the spinal column, without slicing all the way through. Cut through the ligaments of the hindquarters, allowing the legs to be splayed outward.

2 Wash the pig's skin with a damp cloth and shave off the bristles.

3 An hour before grilling, moisten the skin and add salt more generously to the outside than to the inside.

4 While waiting for the fire to take light, place the pig's back against the spit post; attach the hooks of each crossbar to the pig's extremities and secure them with wire. Attach the backbone to the post by passing wire through the vertebrae. The crossbars should be on the backside of the pig, leaving the ribs open to maximum exposure to the heat. This also keeps the pig flat and prevents it from curling in on itself during cooking.

5 Place the spit upright with the ribs facing the fire at a distance that allows for medium heat. Roast on this side for 3 hours. The ribs should brown evenly with no burned spots.

6 When the ribs are well browned, turn the spit 180° and roast another 1 to 2 hours until completely browned. The temperature should be a little lower than during the first stage as the skin browns and burns more quickly than the ribs.

7 Remove the pig from the spit when the skin is golden brown and crispy. Place it on a table, remove the hooks, and begin carving the shoulders and legs. With the ribs facing up, slice between them and serve 2 per person.

Pork Ribs
Costillar de Cerdo

A pig reaches maturity around 175 pounds, which is when its ribs are perfect for grilling. This is the best cut of pork for grilling as the others dry out too easily. Unlike beef, pork should always be well done. Pork ribs have enough fat to ensure that they remain juicy.

Technical Information

WEIGHT: *5 ½ to 8 lbs*

SERVES: *5 to 7 people*

TIME: *1 hour 45 min*

HEAT: *medium*

CHARCOAL: *14 lbs minimum*

Grilling Technique

1 Reduce the fat layer if desired, but do not expose the meat. Add salt or marinade 1 hour before grilling.

2 Place the ribs on the grill, meaty side up, for 1 hour over medium heat. Turn them over and grill the other side for another 45 minutes.

3 Be sure the fat does not burn during this second stage; it should reduce slowly until it becomes a crisp, golden crust that enhances the flavor.

SECRET

PORK IS COOKED WHEN THE MEAT IS JUST SLIGHTLY PINK. IT WILL STILL BE JUICY WHEN CUT. THIS DOES NOT MEAN THAT THE MEAT IS RAW; RAW MEAT IS NOT JUICY.

Sausage
Chorizo or Longaniza

Although most sausages may be cooked on the grill, in South America the most common types are smoked or fresh pork sausages such as "longanizas" and blood sausage. Those made for grilling are smaller, perfect for individual servings. Full-sized sausages may be used, but don't cut them before grilling or they will lose their juice.

Technical Information

WEIGHT: variable
TIME: 30 to 40 min
HEAT: medium
CHARCOAL: 5 lbs minimum

Grilling Technique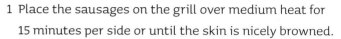

1 Place the sausages on the grill over medium heat for 15 minutes per side or until the skin is nicely browned.
2 Remove them from the grill before the skin wrinkles and breaks open.

SECRET

WHEN GRILLING SAUSAGES OR HOT DOGS FOR A LARGE NUMBER OF GUESTS, TRY THREADING THEM ONTO SINGLE OR DOUBLE SKEWERS, WHICH WILL GREATLY REDUCE THE WORK AT THE GRILL.

Blood Sausage
Morcilla or Prieta

SECRET

BLOOD SAUSAGES ARE PRE-COOKED, SO THEY ONLY NEED TO BE HEATED. THEY SHOULD BE JUICY ON THE INSIDE, SO BE CAREFUL NOT TO OVERCOOK THEM.

Blood sausages come in individual serving sizes and are usually quite easy to grill: just brown them and serve. Don't use a fork to turn them on the grill; use meat tongs to avoid piercing the skin.

Technical Information

TIME: 10 min
HEAT: medium
CHARCOAL: 5 lbs minimum

Grilling Technique

1 Place the sausages on the grill over medium heat. Grill for 10 minutes or until the skin beads with moisture. Carefully rotate their position so that they heat evenly.

2 Remove them from the grill before their skin dries out and breaks.

LAMB AND GOAT

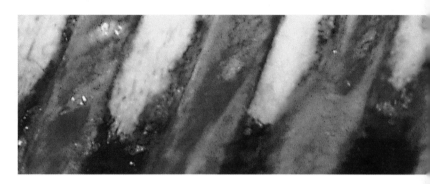

Spit-Roasted Lamb
Cordero al Asador Vertical

The vertical spit was invented especially for grilling Patagonian lamb. Sheep farming is a major economic activity in the Magellan region, and gauchos herding large flocks are a common site. Lamb also makes up a very large part of the local diet. Spring lambs (3 to 6 months old) provide the best meat for spit-roasting; they weigh less than 35 pounds, so their fat covering is moderate and their meat has a delicate flavor. Other options are baby lambs (6 to 8 weeks) or yearlings (12 to 24 months). Mutton (2 years or more) is not recommended for grilling. Any lamb over 6 months will have a heavy layer of fat that must be removed before grilling to reduce the strong flavor. The advantage of the vertical spit is that it reduces the meat's excessive fat as it slowly cooks for 5 or more hours. The meat is cooked by the indirect heat of xthe radiation of the flames and does not require hardwood, which is scarce in this very southern region.

Technical Information

WEIGHT: 18 - 35 lbs

SERVES: 8 - 16 people

TIME: 4 - 5 hours

HARDWOOD: 110 lbs minimum

Grilling Technique

1 To prepare the lamb for flattening and attaching to a vertical spit: Place the animal on its back on a sturdy table. Open its chest with a cleaver or saw and cut out the breastbone to free the rib cage. Create a hinge effect by making a partial cut through the spinal column, without slicing all the way through. Cut through the ligaments of the hindquarters, allowing the legs to be splayed outward.

2 An hour before grilling, moisten the skin and add salt more generously to the outside than to the inside.

3 While waiting for the fire to take light, place the lamb's back against the spit post; attach the hooks of each crossbar to the lamb's extremities and secure them with wire. Attach the backbone to the post by passing wire through the vertebrae. The crossbars should be on the backside of the lamb, leaving the ribs open to maximum exposure to the heat. This also keeps the lamb flat and prevents it from curling in on itself during cooking.

4 Place the spit upright with the ribs facing toward the fire at a distance that allows for medium heat. Roast on this side for 3 hours. The ribs should brown evenly with no burned spots.

5 When the ribs are well-browned, turn the spit 180° and roast another 2 hours until completely browned. The temperature should be a little lower than during the first stage as the skin browns and burns more quickly than the ribs.

6 Remove the lamb from the spit when the skin is golden brown and crispy. Place it on a table, remove the hooks and begin carving the shoulders and legs. With the ribs facing up, slice between them and serve 2 per person.

SECRET
REMOVING THE BREASTBONE BEFORE
PLACING THE LAMB ON THE SPIT
MAKES IT EASIER TO SLICE AND
SERVE THE GRILLED RIBS.

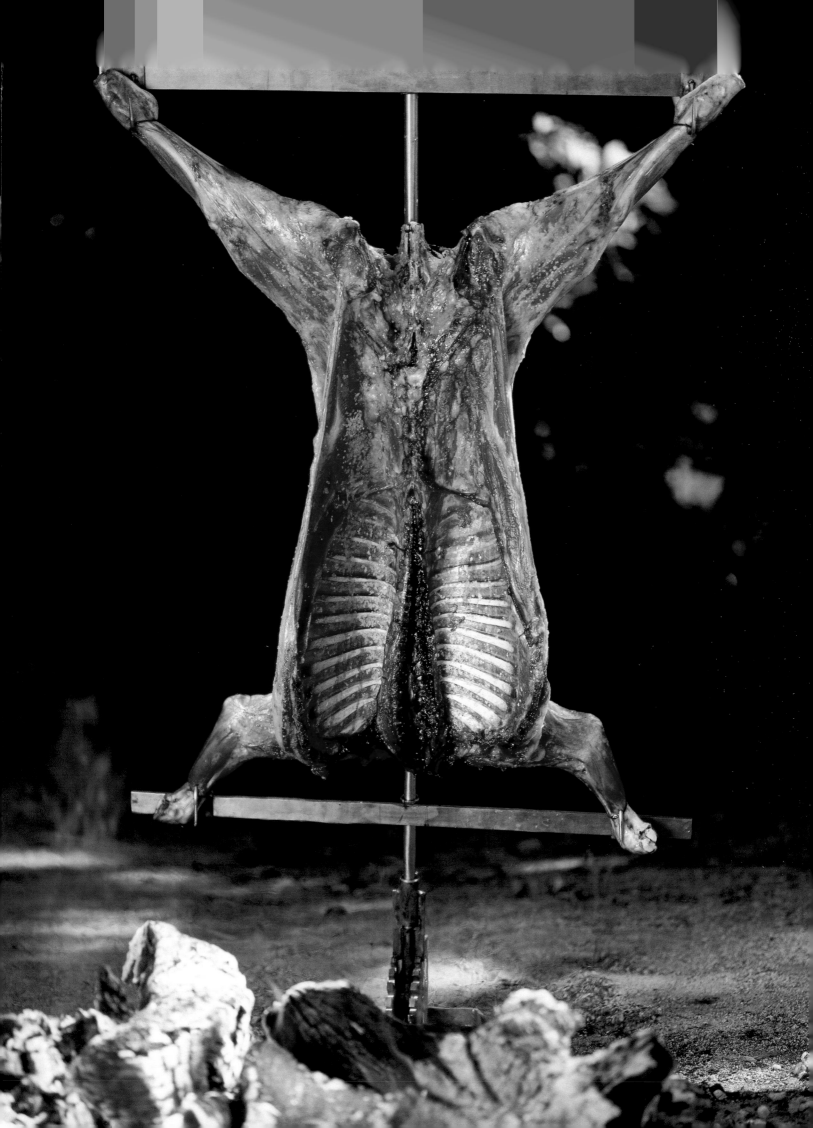

Rack of Lamb
Costillar de Cordero

Lamb is another excellent choice for the grill; all of its cuts contain enough fat for juicy, flavorful meat. Lamb chops are cut from the Rack of Ribs, which consists of 12 bones. Those cut from the first 5 ribs are the most highly-prized because they are the largest and have more marbling than the remaining ribs, which yield the center-cut chops. Shoulders and legs can also be grilled whole or cut against the grain into 1-inch slices. Grill shoulders for 1 hour and legs for 1 ½ hours.

Technical Information

WEIGHT: *1 ½ to 3 ½ lbs*
SERVES: *1 to 2 people*
TIME: *45 min*
HEAT: *medium*
CHARCOAL: *6 lbs minimum*

Grilling Technique

1 Separate the rib cage from the backbone, leaving the loin meat attatched to the ribs.
2 Use a cleaver or saw to trim the ribs to 4 ½ inches in length. Cut the fat covering back, leaving 2 inches of bone exposed.
3 Cut the membrane between the ribs and scrape away the meat to leave the bones clean.
4 Place the full rack of chops on the grill, rib-side down, and roast for 30 minutes over medium heat. Add salt to the fat on the upper side.
5 The meat will have loosened somewhat from the bones and a little foam will appear on the marrow. Turn the chops over to expose the other side for 15 minutes or until brown.
6 Remove the chops from the grill and cut into individual servings: 1 per person as an appetizer and 2 or 3 as the main course.

Spit-Roasted Goat
Chivito or Cabrito al Asador

Young goats (kids) are usually grilled whole in much the same way as lambs, but with shorter cooking times. Suckling goat meat is flavorful and has no intramuscular fat, which makes it very light. Goats raised for meat are kept in corrals, where they are nursed by their mothers when they return from pasture so that the kids do not waste energy following after their mothers. That way they accumulate fat and their musculature remains relaxed. The smallest are 25 days old and weigh 8 pounds. At 45 days they weigh 18 pounds, stop nursing, and leave the corral. The delicate flavor of their tender meat is excellent for grilling and is sure to raise the spirits of all your guests, who will even be tempted to eat it out of hand before it even reaches the plate.

Technical Information

WEIGHT: *9 to 18 lb*
SERVES: *4 to 8 people*
TIME: *1 to 2 hours*
HEAT: *medium*
HARDWOOD: *80 lbs minimum*

Grilling Technique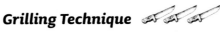

1 The meat of the young goat should be light pink and moderately elastic to the touch (the meat will not spring back immediately when pressed). The interior should have an abundant amount of white fat.

2 An hour before grilling, moisten the surface with water and add moderate amounts of salt to the outside and somewhat less to the inside.

3 While waiting for the fire to take light, place the goat's back against the spit post; attach the hooks of each crossbar to its extremities and secure them with wire. Attach the backbone to the post by passing wire through the vertebrae. The crossbars should be on the backside of the goat, leaving the ribs open to maximum exposure to the heat. This also keeps it flat and prevents it from curling in on itself during cooking.

4 Place the spit upright with the ribs facing toward the fire at a distance that allows for medium heat. Roast on this side for 2 hours. The ribs should brown evenly with no burned spots.

5 When the ribs are well-browned, turn the spit 180° and roast another hour until completely browned. The temperature should be a little lower than during the first stage as the skin browns and burns more quickly than the ribs.

6 Remove the goat from the spit when the skin is golden brown and crispy. Place it on a table, remove the hooks and begin cutting the shoulders and legs. With the ribs facing up, cut between them, serving 2 per person.

SECRET
RUB THE GOAT INSIDE AND OUT WITH THE FOLLOWING MIXTURE AND LET STAND REFRIGERATED FOR 12 TO 24 HOURS:
2 TABLESPOONS OIL
1 TABLESPOON LEMON JUICE
½ TABLESPOON BLACK PEPPER
½ CLOVE GARLIC, CRUSHED
2 TEASPOONS SALT
1 TABLESPOON WATER

CHICKEN

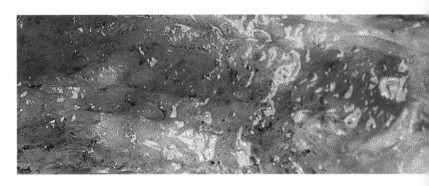

Butterflied Chicken
Pollo Aranado

The most common bird for roasting is the broiler chicken. Its meat is abundant, tender, and mild-flavored. In this technique the chicken is butterflied, or opened to lay flat on the grill. This is an excellent way to grill chicken because it allows the breast and other parts to cook evenly, exposed to the coals on both sides. It is advisable to marinate the chicken for 12 to 24 hours before grilling.

Technical Information

WEIGHT: *4 ½ lbs*

SERVES: *4 people*

TIME: *1 hour 30 min*

HEAT: *medium*

CHARCOAL: *9 lbs minimum*

Grilling Technique

1 Lay the chicken on its back and use a knife or poultry shears to cut along both sides of the chicken until the breast remains joined to the body only by its clavicles and wings. Hold the body against a hard surface with one hand and fold the breast back 180° with the other.

2 Eliminate the excess fat near the tail, but leave the skin intact. Marinate the chicken for 12 to 24 hours, or simply add salt 1 hour before grilling.

3 Place the chicken over the coals, skin-side down, and grill for 45 minutes over medium heat.

4 When the skin is golden, turn the chicken over and grill for an additional 45 minutes on the other side.

5 To serve, place the roasted chicken on a cutting board and use a good knife or kitchen shears to cut it in half lengthwise and then again crosswise, separating the bird into 2 breast-wing quarters and 2 thigh-leg quarters.

SECRET

THE CHICKEN CAN BE MARINATED FOR 12 TO 24 HOURS WITH THE FOLLOWING MARINADE:

2 CLOVES OF GARLIC

2 TABLESPOONS OIL

1 TEASPOON BLACK PEPPER

1 TEASPOON HOT SAUCE

JUICE OF 2 LEMONS

2 TEASPOONS SALT

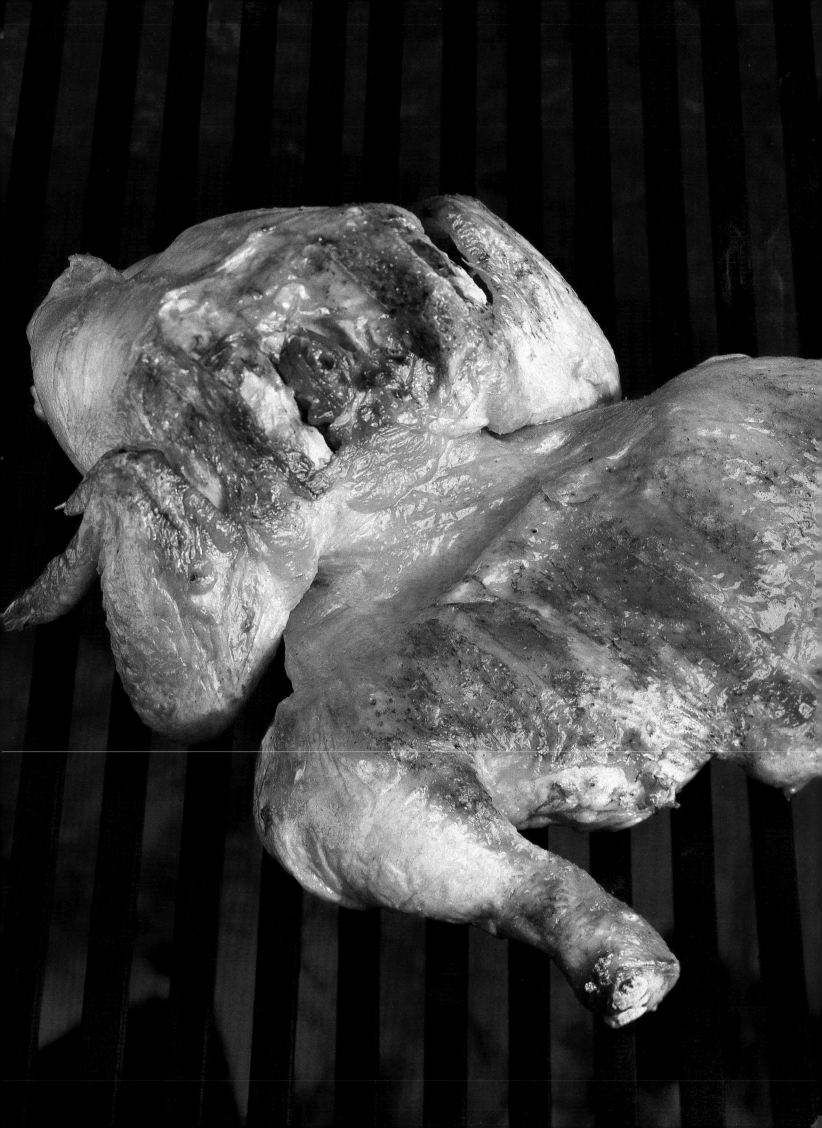

Cornish Hen
Pollo de Grano

Butterfly Cornish hens to grill them whole or prepare them Brazilian-style by cutting them in half and threading them onto skewers. Serve half or a whole chicken per person.

Technical Information

WEIGHT: 1 lb
SERVES: 1 person
TIME: 1 hour
HEAT: medium
CHARCOAL: 7 lbs minimum

Grilling Techniques

ON THE GRILL

1 Use a knife or poultry shears to cut along both sides of the chicken until the breast remains joined to the body only by its clavicles and wings. Open the chicken and fold it back 180°. Marinate for 12 to 24 hours before grilling. If not using a marinade, add salt 1 hour ahead of time.
2 Place the chicken on the grill, skin side down, and cook 30 minutes over medium heat.
3 Once the skin is browned, turn it over and cook another 30 minutes on the other side.
4 To serve, place the chicken on a cutting board and cut it in half lengthwise.

ON A SKEWER

1 Cut the chicken in half lengthwise, leaving a thigh and a wing on each side. The skin may be left on or removed, as desired. For skinless grilling, marinate for 12 to 24 hours before grilling, otherwise, add salt 1 hour ahead of time.
2 Thread the thigh onto the skewer and then the wing for each portion.
3 Place the chicken over the grill, skin side down, and cook 30 minutes over medium heat.
4 Once browned, turn it over and cook another 30 minutes on the other side.

SECRET

MARINATE THE CHICKEN FOR 12 TO 24 HOURS WITH THE FOLLOWING MARINADE:
1 CUP ORANGE JUICE
2 CUPS WHITE WINE
1 ONION, CHOPPED
1 TABLESPOON MUSTARD
1 TABLESPOON FRESH SAGE, MINCED
1 TABLESPOON WHITE PEPPER
2 TEASPOONS SALT

Chicken Thighs, Legs, Wings, Hearts
Muslos, Piernas, Brazos, Corazones

Chicken wings are especially attractive to children as they can eat them out of hand while they play. Thighs and legs are both good alternatives for guests who do not eat red meat. When grilling many wings, thighs, and legs, threading them onto skewers will make it easier to grill them evenly.

Technical Information

TIME: 30 to 60 min

HEAT: medium

CHARCOAL: 7 lbs minimum

HEARTS: these tiny bites are wonderful appetizers when well browned.

WINGS: they may not have much meat, but their crispy, crunchy skin gives them a very nice flavor.

THIGHS AND LEGS: these are the chicken's meatiest and most tender limbs.

Grilling Techniques

HEARTS

1 Eliminate the veins and fat around the heart.
2 Thread the hearts on a skewer and add fine salt. As an alternative, add pieces of bacon between the hearts.
3 Place the hearts on the grill over medium heat for 30 minutes until they are well browned.
4 Remove the hearts from the skewers. Serve with toothpicks and your choice of dipping sauces.

THIGHS, LEGS, AND WINGS

1 Insert a skewer through the center of the pieces and add fine salt. Wings cook faster than thighs and legs, so don't place them together on the same skewers.
2 Place the skewers on the grill over medium heat until the chicken is well browned: 15 minutes per side for wings and 30 minutes per side for thighs and legs.

SECRET

FLARE-UPS ARE A TYPICAL PROBLEM WHEN GRILLING CHICKEN, BUT THE SOLUTION IS SIMPLE: START BY PUTTING THE SKIN SIDE DOWN OVER THE COALS TO SEAL IN THE JUICE AND FAT.

VENISON AND BOAR

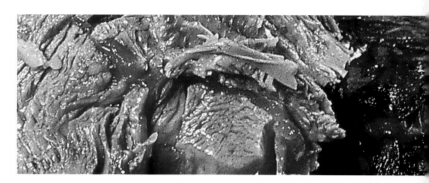

Spit-Roasted Venison
Ciervo al Palo

Deer were first introduced in Patagonia around 1880 when the Gamo Deer was first brought to Chile's 9th and 10th Regions. Red Deer were added in 1930, and the Corzo Deer some time later. This delicious lean meat has an attractive red color and a wild taste that increases with age. Young deer less than 6 months old are remarkably tender. Venison should be grilled just to rare; the meat dries out and toughens very quickly when overcooked. Meat from adult deer is best prepared in the kitchen using typical recipes for European stews.

Technical Information

WEIGHT: *45 to 65 lbs*
SERVES: *25 people*
TIME: *4 hours*
HEAT: *medium*
HARDWOOD: *110 lbs minimum*

Grilling Technique

1 Prepare to grill the venison rotisserie-style on a horizontal spit by cutting the deer in half lengthwise with a saw. Insert each half onto a long metal rod or a wooden shaft cut from a straight and sturdy young tree. Moisten the surface of the meat with water and apply salt.

2 Place the rod over the supports anchored in the ground with sufficient height so that the heat that reaches the meat will be medium. Keep the fire slightly away from the meat to avoid smoke and to cook it by indirect radiant heat.

3 Begin with the ribs facing the heat for 15 to 20 minutes and then rotate the spit. Continue rotating the meat every 20 minutes for 3 to 4 hours.

4 Remove the venison from the spit, place it on a table and begin carving the meat by cutting the shoulders and legs. Then place the ribs face up, slice between them, and serve 2 per person.

SECRET
BRUSH THE VENISON PERIODICALLY
WITH OIL OR LARD WHILE GRILLING
FOR A NICE GOLDEN COLOR AND TO
AVOID BURNING THE SURFACE.

Spit-Roasted Boar

Jabalí al Asador Vertical

Fortunately for those of us who like boar meat but don't want to come face-to-face with one in the woods, today there are many breeders who supply restaurants and game-lovers alike. The advantage of buying farm-grown meats is that the producers know when the animals are mating and can avoid butchering them during those periods when the meat is full of unpleasant odors. Furthermore, regular balanced feeding produces splendid boars with a greater proportion of fat than their wild counterparts, which often fast for prolonged periods. If you decide to prepare a boar on the grill, or better yet, on a vertical spit, choose a young, 5 to 8-month-old farm-raised animal with a live weight of no more than 90 pounds.

Technical Information

WEIGHT: 45 to 65 lbs
SERVES: 25 people
TIME: 4 to 5 hours
HEAT: medium
HARDWOOD: 90 lbs minimum

Grilling Technique

1 To prepare the young boar for flattening and attaching to a vertical spit: Place the boar on its back on a sturdy table. Open its chest with a cleaver or saw and cut out the breastbone to free the rib cage. Make a partial cut through the spinal column, without slicing all the way through, for a hinge effect. Cut through the ligaments of the hindquarters, allowing the legs to be splayed outward.

2 Clean the skin with a damp cloth and shave off its bristles.

3 An hour before grilling, moisten the skin and add salt generously to the outside and somewhat less on the inside.

4 While waiting for the fire to take light, place the boar's back against the spit post; attach the hooks of each crossbar to its extremities and secure them with wire. Attach the backbone to the post by passing wire through the vertebrae. The crossbars should be on the backside of the animal, leaving the ribs open to maximum exposure to the heat. This also keeps the boar flat and prevents it from curling in on itself during cooking.

5 Place the spit upright with the ribs facing toward the fire at a distance that allows for medium heat. Roast on this side for 3 hours. The ribs should brown evenly with no burned spots.

6 When the ribs are well-browned, turn the spit 180º and roast another hour until completely browned. The temperature should be a little lower than during the first stage as the skin browns and burns more quickly than the ribs.

7 Remove the boar from the spit when the skin is golden brown and crispy. Place it on a table, remove the hooks and begin cutting the shoulders and legs. With the ribs facing up, slice between them, serving 2 per person.

SECRET

BOAR IS LEANER THAN PORK AND SO WILL COOK FASTER, EVEN THOUGH THE ANIMAL MAY BE LARGER.

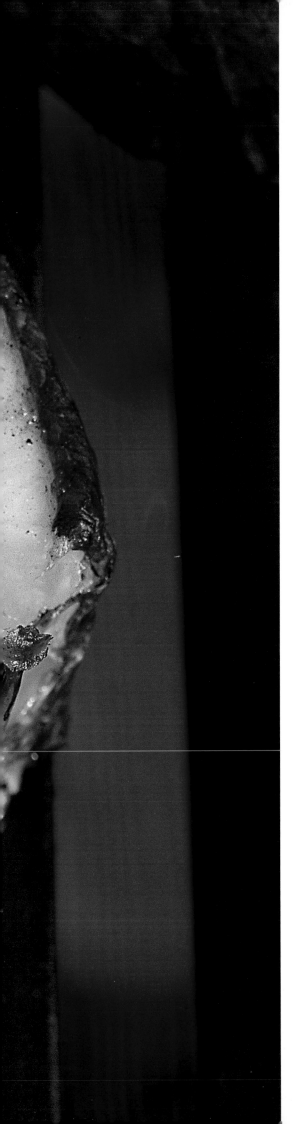

FISH

Trout
Trucha

Trout are beautiful freshwater cousins of salmon and can reach up to 3 feet in length. The orange-colored meat is firm-textured, flavorful, and slightly oily. Farmed trout are harvested when they reach a weight of approximately 1 ½ pounds. Chilean Patagonia is world-famous for the quality and quantity of the trout found in it many lakes and rivers.

Technical Information

WEIGHT: *1 ¼ lbs*

SERVES: *1 person*

TIME: *15 min*

HEAT: *medium-high*

CHARCOAL: *5 lbs minimum*

Grilling Technique

1 Use kitchen shears to remove the fins from the previously cleaned and gutted fish. Enlarge and deepen the abdominal incision from the head to the tail, and remove the abdominal bones where they enter the spine so it can be flattened.

2 Season with lemon, salt, and black pepper. Other seasonings may be used, but be careful not to overpower the very delicate flavor of the fish.

3 Place the fish skin-side down over the coals at medium heat for 15 minutes. Trout meat is very fragile, so use a grill basket to prevent it from breaking.

4 Brush often with melted butter. The meat will turn from dark pink to light pink as it cooks.

5 To serve, carefully remove the trout from the grill and place it directly on the serving plate. The bones will have loosened during the cooking process and your guests can easily remove them as they eat.

Salmon
Salmón

This beautiful oval-shaped fish can grow to more than 3 feet in length. It has a bluish-colored back and a silver belly with an iridescent shimmer along the sides. Males also have red or orange spots. The orange-colored meat is firm and oily. There are many species indigenous to both the Atlantic and the Pacific Oceans, and all swim upriver to spawn. Chile very successfully farms the Atlantic variety and has become a world-leader in the large-scale production of outstanding quality salmon. Farmed salmon are harvested at approximately 8 pounds. Their small silver scales bond firmly to the skin when heated, so it is not necessary to remove them before grilling.

Technical Information

WEIGHT: 4 to 8 lbs

SERVES: 5 to 10 people

TIME: 40 min

HEAT: medium-high

CHARCOAL: 9 lbs minimum

Grilling Technique

1 Use kitchen shears to remove the fins from the previously cleaned and gutted fish. Enlarge the abdominal incision from the head to the tail and fill the interior with fresh sage and basil leaves, salt, pepper, and butter. Place additional sage leaves on the outside and wrap the fish with cotton kitchen string. The sage will release a delicious aroma while cooking.

2 Place the salmon in a fish-grilling basket and place over medium-high heat, 20 minutes per side or until golden brown.

3 To serve, cut the string and use a spatula to remove the meat, beginning near the head and working toward the tail. Work around the bones to avoid serving them.

SECRET
BRUSH THE SKIN WITH MELTED
BUTTER AND LEMON JUICE FOR A
BEAUTIFUL GOLDEN COLOR.

Grouper
Mero or Dorado

The Grouper can reach up to 3 feet in length and has a flat, oval-shaped body. It has a large head and many teeth, gills adorned with 3 needles, and a strong tail. Its fierce character is reflected in its Spanish name "Mero," which is derived from the Latin "Nero," the ruthless Roman Emperor. Its much-appreciated meat is considered one of the most flavorful and best for grilling as it has a firm texture and is moderately fatty.

Technical Information

THICKNESS: *2 inches*

WEIGHT: *¾ to 1 ¼ lbs*

SERVES: *1 to 2 people*

TIME: *20 min*

HEAT: *medium*

CHARCOAL: *6 lbs minimum*

Grilling Technique

1 Slice the fish into 2-inch steaks and add salt to both sides.

2 Lightly grease the grill to prevent sticking before adding the steaks.

3 Place the steaks over the coals at medium heat for 15 minutes per side or until they are lightly browned.

4 The skin softens with the heat and becomes very fragile. To serve, use grill tongs and a metal spatula to carefully pick up each steak by the outer sides, which are protected by the skin. Serve one per person.

SECRET
LEAVE THE SKIN INTACT
TO PRESERVE THE SHAPE
OF THE STEAK.

EVERYTHING ELSE

EVERYTHING ELSE

Thirst seems to go hand in hand with grilling. Just starting the fire and the anticipation of what is to come is enough to set our salivary glands in action! So light the fire, open a bottle, and let the event begin!

DRINKS

The only true "aperitifs" or "before dinner drinks" are those that stimulate the appetite and start the gastric juices flowing. Forget about overly sweet drinks as they have the opposite effect. Distilled spirits such as whisky and gin are also out because their high alcohol content deadens the taste buds and irritates the stomach. The ideal drink before a meal should be slightly bitter, moderately acidic, and have a low alcohol content, such as beer and wine.

BEER: Nothing hits the spot better than a nice cold beer to fend off the thirst that comes with the heat of the grill. It tends to be low in alcohol, slightly bitter, and have a thirst-quenching effect that works miracles for bringing on an appetite. Pilsners and lighter beer should be served at 42° to 50°F and dark beer at 50° to 54°F.

WINE: Red wine is the traditional drink of choice in Patagonia. A little wine whets the appetite, helps digestion, and gets the gastric juices flowing as it stimulates conversation and warms the hearts of your guests. Wine is considered the healthiest of all alcoholic beverages. The astringency of hearty red wines such as Cabernet Sauvignon, Syrah, Carmenère, or Malbec is produced by their tannins, which also have the benefit of being loaded with antioxidants.

CHOOSING THE RIGHT WINE: When it comes time to fire up the grill, Cabernet Sauvignon is a favorite. In fact, professional wine tasters often use the term "meaty" to describe these big, hearty wines that generally make excellent companions for grilled meats. They aren't the only option however; there are a number of alternatives to choose from. Here are some suggestions:

BEEF AND GAME: oak-aged Cabernet Sauvignon, Syrah and Malbec. Serve at 60° to 64°F.

PORK: oak-aged Merlot and Carmenère. Serve at 57° to 60°F.

LAMB AND GOAT: oak-aged Malbec and Syrah. Serve at 57° to 60°F.

CHICKEN: Merlot and Carmenère. Serve at 57° to 60°F.

GAME: oak-aged Syrah, Malbec, and Cabernet Sauvignon. Serve at 60° to 64°F.

OILY FISH: oak-aged Chardonnay and Pinot Noir. Serve at 54° to 57°F.

VARIETY MEATS, SAUSAGES, AND HOT DOGS: These foods include a wide variety of spices and generally combine better with white wines than red. Try Sauvignon Blanc, Riesling, or an unwooded Chardonnay. People with more traditional tastes may appreciate an older Semillon. Serve at 43° to 50°F.

WINE SERVICE: There are a few basic factors to consider to really appreciate the wine. First, it should be opened correctly and served at the right temperature in order to best express its character. Many wines will improve with oxygen, but the idea that wine should be opened early and left "to breathe" is not as useful as many people believe. A full bottle of wine has very little contact with the air and will in fact improve much more quickly once poured into a glass than it will in an hour in the bottle, so open your bottle when you are ready to serve it.

"PEBRES" AND "SALSAS"

These culinary complements are bold and spicy combinations of raw vegetables and seasonings designed to stimulate both appetite and thirst. The vegetable components in salsas are finely chopped or lightly ground with a mortar and pestle, and their thick consistency prevents them from running. Typical Patagonian salsas are called "pebres," a name derived from their essential ingredient, pepper. The first "pebres" arrived with the Conquistadors who brought pepper, onions, green onions, garlic, cilantro, parsley, and oregano to the New World. These ingredients were combined with the tomatoes, chilies, and green peppers indigenous to the region and quickly gave rise to the new American cuisine.

CHILI-GARLIC SALSA: Seeded green chili peppers, garlic, and whole black pepper ground in a mortar and mixed with oil, lemon juice or white vinegar, and salt.

"CRIOLLA" SALSA: There are any number of variations of this sauce. The flavors and lively colors of red and green bell peppers and tomatoes predominate in the salsa and are complemented with onion, extra-virgin olive oil, red wine vinegar, fresh parsley, and a little salt and pepper. All the ingredients are painstakingly chopped and then mixed with the seasonings. A sprinkling of finely-chopped parsley tops this very typical creation.

DRIED CHILI PEPPER PEBRE: This is a simple salsa that mixes seeded dried red chili peppers with onion or green onion, cilantro and garlic. Chop everything well and add fresh-ground black pepper, red-wine vinegar, oil, and salt.

CILANTRO AND TOMATO PEBRE: Much-loved throughout the Americas, this salsa is made of cilantro, green onions, garlic, ground chili pepper, and firm, peeled tomatoes. Chop everything well and add black pepper, red wine vinegar, oil, and salt.

CHIMICHURRI SALSA: A classic from Argentina, ideal for topping grilled beef and lamb. The basic ingredients are 5 cloves of garlic, crushed; 4 bay leaves, ground; 3 heaping tablespoons oregano; 1 teaspoon coarsely ground black pepper; 4 tablespoons ground chili pepper; 4 tablespoons olive oil, and 1 cup of red wine vinegar. Grind the ingredients together, place in a bottle or jar, shake vigorously, and leave in a cool, dark place for a week before using.

 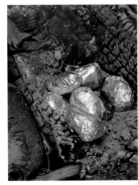

POTATOES AND GRILLED ONIONS ARE FAVORITES AT ANY BARBECUE. THEIR MILD FLAVORS NICELY COMPLEMENT GRILLED MEATS AND THEY ARE EASY TO PREPARE, SO SUCCESS IS PRACTICALLY GUARANTEED.

SIDE DISHES

Balance is the key to this gustatory orgy. While some side dishes are provocative and exciting, such as salsas with onion, garlic, and chili peppers, others, such as potatoes and grilled eggplant help calm the taste buds and tame strong flavors.

POTATOES: The mild flavor of potatoes is an excellent way to neutralize the stronger flavors of the other dishes on the table. Wrap them in aluminum foil, lay them into the embers, cover them with hot ashes, and let them bake for 40 minutes. To serve, remove the foil and cut them in half.

ONIONS: Roast whole onions with their skins among the coals of a hot fire for 30 to 45 minutes, depending on their size. When they are soft to the touch, remove them from the fire and allow them to cool. Brush them off and peel away the charred skins, being careful not to contaminate them with ashes or burnt skin. Cut the onions into small pieces; they will separate into soft, juicy, aromatic layers. Dress them with olive oil, salt, and lemon juice.

LETTUCE: The king of all salad vegetables comes in many varieties and a wide range of flavors and textures that combine wonderfully with all types of grilled meats. Add the dressing just before serving, and keep it simple; try tossing the lettuce with olive oil, fresh-squeezed lemon juice, salt, and pepper.

EGGPLANT: Originally from the Far East, eggplants are ideal for an appetizer or side dish at a barbecue; their slightly spicy flavor is a wonderful complement for beef, lamb, or pork. Slice them into rounds for appetizers and in half for a side dish; drizzle them in olive oil, sprinkle with salt, oregano, and chili pepper, and grill for 30 minutes over medium heat.

GRILLED VEGETABLES: A griller's imagination can run wild when it comes to vegetables. Simply placed on the grill or on skewers, their aromas and flavors transform them into a welcome addition to the table. Cut the onions, peppers, and tomatoes in half and alternate them on skewers or a serving platter for a colorful presentation.

"CHANCHO EN PIEDRA": A classic "pebre" made with peeled and chopped ripe tomato, garlic, fresh cilantro, oregano, and green chili pepper all ground together in a large stone mortar and pestle and seasoned with oil and salt.

THE BEST SIDE DISHES ARE THOSE THAT CAN BE PREPARED DURING THE BARBECUE WITHOUT HAVING TO ENTER THE KITCHEN. PUTTING YOUR GUESTS TO WORK WILL HELP CALM THE ANXIETY OF WAITING.

Typical Patagonian desserts tend to be sweet, rich, and full of caramel and cream. While they may be delicious, they are very high in calories and do not aid in digestion. Choose refreshing desserts for a barbecue.

DESSERTS

Sorbets, fresh fruit, and even grilled fruit are ideal desserts to bring a rich barbecue to a delicious close.

ROASTED CINNAMON BANANAS: Place large, ripe, unpeeled bananas directly on the grill over medium heat until the peels are completely blackened and start to open. Remove the bananas from the grill and place them on a serving platter. Carefully cut both ends and open the peel but do not remove the banana. Sprinkle them with cinnamon and serve one per person. Be sure to make extras because your guests will certainly ask for seconds!

"PAPAYA ALEGRE": This traditional dessert is the ideal ending for a hearty barbecue because papayas have a natural enzyme that aids digestion. Canned papayas are more convenient because fresh papayas are difficult to peel and the digestive enzyme can irritate your hands during the preparation. Place a whole or chopped papaya in an individual dessert dish. Seprately, mix the papaya juice with orange juice and a dash of pisco or white wine. Pour the juice mixture over the papaya and garnish with a dollop of whipped cream.

GRILLED PINEAPPLES: Pineapples are one of the few fruits that can be prepared on the grill with amazing results. Peel a ripe pineapple and sprinkle it with a little rum. Insert a skewer and place it over the coals for 20 minutes as the barbecue is winding down. The advantage of using skewers is that you won't need to clean the grease off the grill before grilling. Cut the pineapple into bite-sized chunks and be prepared to take a bow; your guests are sure to applaud your multi-faceted grilling skills!

AFTER DINNER DRINKS

Those who know how to eat well prefer to save a glass of the last wine for the perfect after-dinner drink. Just when the taste-buds are tired and half asleep, pour a glass of hearty red wine. It will turn velvety smooth as it softly warms in your mouth and cleanses away the last traces of dessert.

DISTILLED SPIRITS: The healthiest and most digestible spirits are those made from grapes, such as Cognac, Brandy, and oak-aged Pisco. Other spirits such as Whisky and "Añejo" Rums and Tequilas are also good alternatives. Avoid sweet and sugary liqueurs as they do not help digestion.

CIGARS: For the perfect ending to a successful barbecue, nothing beats a good Cuban cigar.

RECIPE INDEX

DEGREE OF DIFFICULTY

The recipes presented in this book have been selected for easy preparation by any home cook, although some require more time and skill than others. The following scale indicates the degree of difficulty of preparation of each dish:

Fast and easy.

Moderately easy.

Requires more time and attention during preparation.

SECRETS OF THE
PATAGONIAN BARBECUE
Is an ORIGO book

Recipes by
Roberto Marín, Héctor Salagado, and
Hernán Maino

www.patagonianbarbecue.com

* * *
Managing Editor
Hernán Maino

Consulting Editor
George Luksic

Editor
Margaret Snook

Photography
Rafael Fernández

Graphic Production
Alejandro Torres

* * *

Copyright © 2005 Origo Ediciones
Registration N° 148,320
ISBN 956-8077-32-4

Printed by Quebecor World Chile S.A.

ORIGO CHILE
Padre Alonso de Ovalle 748
6510159, Santiago, Chile
Tel (56-2) 638 8399 • Fax (56-2) 638 3565
www.origo.cl

ORIGO ARGENTINA
Lavalle 1634 - 3° G
C1048AAN, Buenos Aires, Argentina
Tel (54-11) 4374 1456 • Fax (54-11) 4373 0669

THE WINE APPRECIATION GUILD
360 Swift Avenue
South San Francisco CA 94080
1-800-231-9463
www.wineappreciation.com